D1391318

OF WIND AND WATER

OF WIND AND WATER

A Kiwi Pilot in Coastal Command

James Sanders

Airlife
England

Copyright © James Sanders, 1989

British Library Cataloguing in Publication Data
Sanders, James, *1911–*
    Of wind and water.
    1.   World War 2. Air operations by Great Britain.
    Royal Air Force. Fighter operations. Pilots —
    biographies
    I.   Title
    940.54'4941'0924

    ISBN 1-85310-069 2

First published in the UK 1989
by Airlife Publishing Ltd.

Printed in England by Livesey Ltd., Shrewsbury.

Airlife Publishing Ltd.

101 Longden Road, Shrewsbury, England.

Contents

Foreword

There's no need to tell me I am biased in support of James Sanders' writing. I am. And I admit it.

I have long thought that to recapture, nearly fifty years on, the ethos of the air war requires of an author two principal attributes: first, he must himself have experienced all the sensations which were a part of operational flying — anticipation, doubt, fear, sudden shock and elation — and be sympathetic with the private traumas which overtook aircrew when they faced mortal danger. Most of them (because they were all volunteers and naturally imbued with a 'press-on' spirit) outwardly made light of the risks. That was the façade. The silent, personal battle went on behind. Because the author is not inhibited from sharing the inner frailties of his wartime colleagues, he lets the reader into the secret thoughts which most kept hidden from the public gaze.

Extrovert bravado and the stiff upper lip never fooled James Sanders.

Second, the writer must be able, by his descriptive power, to take the reader behind the external wall. For success, he must be capable of making operations live as they once concentrated the minds of his comrades. It is not easy. So often descriptions tend to be no more than a recitation of the commonplace and the obvious.

The author of the story which follows has these two assets in enviable measure. You will find nothing banal in his accounts of the epoch through which he passed. He has the trained, objective eye of the first-rate journalist. He sees things now as acutely as he once experienced them and he can reproduce them because he writes at first hand in compellingly direct and simple prose. His writing penetrates to the truth.

Reading this autobiographical story has reminded me of a telling little exchange between Sherlock Holmes and a Mr James M Dodd, 'a big, fresh, sunburnt, upstanding Briton,' in the tale of *The Blanched Soldier*. Mr Dodd is no longer able to hide his astonishment at the great detective's power of observation and analysis:

'Mr Holmes,' he exclaims, 'you are a wizard ... You see everything.'

The compliment is brushed curtly aside. 'I see no more than you,' retorts Holmes, 'but I have trained myself to notice what I see.'

James Sanders saw it all and it stuck. His advantage is that, having seen and absorbed it, he can now, through his pen, recapture the past — and make it live.

I'll be surprised if you disagree.

London
July, 1989

Laddie Lucas, CBE, DSO, DFC

Prologue

Once, when I was young, there was a war. And when, on 3 September 1939, the New Zealand Government of the day declared its involvement in the affair, my mate Toby Webster and I volunteered to fly with the Royal New Zealand Air Force, should that service require our assistance.

I think that at first we were moved more by the spirit of adventure, a need to validate our manhood, perhaps, than by the burnings of patriotism. But after we had been accepted as trainee pilots and grew to know our commitments, loyalty shone bright.

I was fascinated by flight. It was an entanglement that became a haunting, love-hate relationship, so that no matter how much I was humiliated and hurt, I always returned for more pain. But there was a great pleasure so often awaiting me. Ah, that pleasure was worth it all!

Certainly, the times and events of that period of service life were significant. Many of my experiences were shared by countless other young pilots from various lands, who were destined to survive the war years without trailing streamers of glory in their homecomings. Our consciences were secure in the knowledge that we had at least tried to perform what was expected of us to the best of our abilities.

I have been looking at yellowing photographs and leafing through some old documents; and it is with lingering wonder that I re-discover that my last solo flight was on 10 October 1950. The aircraft was a Harvard trainer of the RNZAF — old NZ1017, to be precise — and my chore was to tow a drogue air-to-air target for my fellow pilots of 1 (Auckland) Territorial Squadron to try to hit.

I say the wonder lingers; because, for the life of me, I do not know how the intervening years have slipped by so quickly. Almost every entry in my flying log-books is evocative of the times, the places, the men and the machines. It is probably because Air Force requirements demanded a prompt and succinct diary notation of every flight completed. The bare facts, in indelible ink, can become engraved deep in the subconscious. For the act of flight, won by wingless man over nature's endeavours to hold humanity earthbound, impassions.

The wonder, the magic and the tragedies hang there somewhere in timeless storage, close to the surface of tingling, total recall. They await a word, a sign, a sound that will bring them, burning bright, into the here-and-now.

Flight challenges and excites, because two of its handmaidens are Fear and Death. Nor are these harpies unknown on land or on sea; but they strike more quickly in the air. Fear is the progeny of man's troubled mind. Death is the daughter of Fate.

Their siren calls troubled and challenged me, a fatalistic fellow who was fearful of being afraid; and through the tumbling years I have continued to squabble with Fear while calling on Luck, a very good friend of mine, to help stay the advances of Death.

I would guess, with accuracy no doubt, that every flying man I have met has known fear in the air. It can be a mercifully brief phase or it can be a cumulative thing.

It begins in surprise. Perhaps, of a sudden, an engine may cut out. With quick reflexes the pilot feathers the propeller, his nerves tingling and the adrenalin beginning to flow. But when the flames stream out from under the engine cowling, his guts grow cold and he stabs at the fire-extinguisher button. Now he is, but yet, only startled. He is probably not in full fright until his flight engineer tells him that, to add to his troubles, the fuel supply at the extremity of the ocean patrol, is now dangerously low.

It is during the long, nerve-plucking haul homeward across dark waters that imagination builds up the suspense, and fear begins to grow. The pilot may shake it off when the home runway comes in sight. But it may, by now, be rooted like a cancer. His nerves may have had more than their share of other alarms.

This fear may manifest itself in later flights. The man's landings will be more perilous, with bounces and over-shoots frequently attending the homecomings. His lips will be dry and his feet will jiggle and judder, like those of a palsy sufferer, on the rudder pedals as he makes his final approach and flare-out. On take-offs he may sometimes allow his aircraft to get into a swing — so much so, perhaps, that he will have to throttle back and make another attempt to get airborne. His breath will be sour and his body will exude the smell of the hunted and the haunted.

I have known it all — the churning belly, the dry mouth and the nagging, doubt-ridden double flight check before take-off, fearful that I might have mis-trimmed the elevators, or left undone those things which I ought to have done. I don't know, other than the occasional rest from flying, what the prescribed cure for fear is. Some are more susceptible to the disease than others. I suffered a lot. I suppose I knew, from the earliest days of my Air Force training, that I did not rate a prominent place in the front ranks of the bold. But I aspired to courage and tried to emulate those who had that shining quality.

I have always been stirred by the exploits and the moral hardihood of Captain Robert Falcon Scott and his band of Antarctic explorers. Scott's personal friend, the renowned James M Barrie of *Peter Pan* fame, mentioned the spirit of those ill-starred travellers in a rectorial address he delivered at St Andrews University, Scotland, in 1922.

I bought a paperback copy of that address, *Courage*, in 1940 and it became a source of quiet guidance. I carried it amongst my gear through every war theatre that had the doubtful benefit of my involvement. It has come back from its kit-bag travels along the countless landing strips of Egypt, the bomb-pocked airfields of Malta and the various Air Force stations I inhabited throughout Britain. I have the little book today, its blue paper cover torn and patched together with scotch tape. But its message is as clear and as needed now as it was more than seventy-five years ago. Barrie quotes, in part, Captain Scott's personal message to him:

> 'We are pegged out in a very comfortless spot. Hoping this letter may be found and sent to you, I write a word of farewell. I want you to think well of me and my end . . . Goodbye — I am not at all afraid of the end, but sad to miss many a simple pleasure which I had planned for the future in our long marches . . . We are in a desperate state — feet frozen, no fuel and a long way from food. But it would do your heart good to be in our tent to hear our songs and our cheery conversations . . . We are very near the end . . . We did intend to finish ourselves when things proved like this, but we have decided to die naturally.'

So — all who fly know fear!

All, in time, will know death. But the tragedy and pity is that so many have gone, and will continue to go, each to his own certain star so young. Toby Webster, who sank his Albemarle off the end of the runway at Gibraltar; Les Norman, my Baltimore navigator from London, who one day flew with another crew — and did not return from a patrol off the island of Gavhdos; Allan Parker, whose Mosquito's wooden wing spar collapsed in full flight after it had been weakened by Asian termites; Howie Schraeder from Canada, whose Blenheim crashed and burned at Bicester. The list, it seems, is endless. There were so many.

Maurice Maeterlinck was a Belgian writer who held the conviction that no man dies so long as he dwells in the memory of those who love him. His hauntingly beautiful play *The Blue Bird* tells of the children, Mytyl and Tyltyl, in search of happiness. Shepherded by Light, they explore the Past and the Future, the Palace of Night and the Kingdom of the Dead and of the Unborn. They find themselves in a graveyard; and Mytyl grows fearful of her first contact with the great mystery of Death.

But the graveyard, with its wooden crosses and grass-covered mounds, is moonlit and tranquil; and of a sudden, as the magic diamond is turned in Tyltyl's fingers, even the tombstones and all the grand investiture of death disappear, to be replaced by luxuriant, swaying clusters of lilies.

'Where are the dead?' asks Mytyl in amazement, searching for traces of even one tombstone.

Her brother also looks. 'There are no dead,' he replies.

I look at my old log-books. As I turn the pages, as Tyltyl turned the revealing diamond in his fingers, the names come alive again. And so long as they continue to dwell so gently in my mind, I know there are no dead.

I should like to recount the tales of some of these young men, so that the telling may give them re-born life and lustre — an immortality, maybe, that they never expected. I could tell, too, of some of the aircraft and the missions they flew; and of the bright blue sky that beckoned them from above the overcast of earthly affairs.

I should like to tell you of luck, that sometimes flew as a silent invisible crew member on some amazing sorties. And I will have to speak, too, of ugly misfortune that somehow managed to ship aboard too many flights and confound the most careful ministrations of aircraft fitters and riggers.

And I'll tell again of fate.

A certain occasion at Gianaclis comes to mind.

Gianaclis, whatever that place might be now, was, in October 1942, an RAF airstrip on the fringe of the Nile Delta. While the British Eighth Army gathered itself for the coming storm at El Alamein, 203 Squadron, RAF, was renewing its strength with more Maryland and Baltimore reconnaissance machines after being chased out of Burg el Arab by Rommel's eastward drive.

I sat in my tent, writing a letter home. The day was warm and the sky was cloudless. Westward, on the edge of the flying field, were the aircraft maintenance tents and from that direction came the rising and falling roars of Pratt & Whitney engines answering to their ground tests.

My flight commander sent a messenger to find me. I was to take Maryland G-George on a test flight, now that her ground crew had done their repair work on the motors.

'Goddamn,' I complained, 'I'm right in the middle of this letter.'

Sergeant-pilot Vailland, close at hand, spoke up: 'I'll take her, if you like,' he offered. 'I want to build up my flying hours.'

'I don't give a damn who flies the bloody thing, so long as the aircraft is tested,' the flight commander shrugged when Vailland put the proposition to him.

Vailland re-appeared soon, lumping his parachute harness and dangling his flying helmet by its intercom flexes. He was grinning. 'You know,' he said to me, 'I can't get enough of these trips.

I had finished my letter when I heard the Maryland being gunned for take-off; and as it tore with full power into the wind and roared overhead, a staccato of explosions brought us scrambling from our tents to see a stream of black smoke trailing from the port engine. In horror we watched the sick Maryland vomit more and more fumes and flame, and waited for the pilot to set the machine down and make an escape bid before the holocaust. But now he was flying over the delta's jungle of palm trees and paddy-field irrigation ditches.

The aircraft was sinking lower and the fire was now well out of control. And just before it disappeared from view it turned to port. Vailland had probably found a spot to belly-flop the Maryland.

We waited a moment or two in deepening gloom. And soon a ball of smoke, so black and thick that it seemed to be of some solid, evil substance, rose above the spidery, heat-dancing fringe of palms on the skyline. Meanwhile, some of the squadron's MT trucks had been started and were already rumbling off towards the crash, following the wheel-tracks of the fire tender.

The smoke rose in a high black pillar and the fire burned for a long time. It was late afternoon before one of the trucks brought in the victims that Maryland G-George had carried in her passenger list.

Demonstrating sublime confidence in their skills and handiwork, four aircraftmen and their sergeant responsible for the mechanical and general airworthiness of the aeroplane had begged a joy-ride of the pilot. All of the six in G-George were badly burnt. They were alive when they reached the camp, but through the night the five ground-crew boys died.

I visited Vailland when he lay in hospital in Alexandria. He was very ill and his burnt flesh filled the room with the stench of putrefaction. The heroics of aircraft fires are the stuff of Hollywood — the real flames strip a crash of any vestige of glamour.

He asked, softly: 'How are the others?'

'I don't know,' I lied. 'They got out alive, though.'

'They are alive now, aren't they?' He begged desperately for my assurance.

'I don't know. Yes — yes, I'm sure they are,' I shuffled and stammered. 'But I'm on leave, so I'm a bit out of touch. I'm off to Malta soon. I came from Gianaclis without knowing.'

Vailland looked at me reproachfully. Although he wanted to hear that the boys had survived the crash, he didn't want to hear a lie or a half-lie. I had wanted to ease his conscience. I had not succeeded. My evasions had been transparent.

I stood indicted in that hospital which smelt of death. If I had flown that test flight it would have been me lying there, swathed in bandages and stinking of the body's corruption. Either way, the ground-crew fellows would probably still be dead. But Vailland would be unharmed, still looking for more flights to bolster up the totals in his log-book.

I do not know if Vailland survived. But he was looking very ill that day I visited him in hospital. I went off to Malta and so beyond the ken of the men of 203 Squadron and their flying affairs in Egypt.

Fear and death — and luck — went along with me.

1
A Piece of Cake

The nine sergeants who made up the audience outside the flight hut at Luqa, Malta, hung on the wing commander's words like a covey of open-beaked fledgelings eager for nourishment. The officer stuttered somewhat, so the young flyers — who constituted three complete but very raw Blenheim crews in transit from Britain to the Middle East — were able to swallow patiently the syllables and digest them slowly, even if the food, intelligence-wise, was rather light in calories.

'You f-fly south from here until you s-strike the coast of un-un-North Africa,' he directed.

The sergeant-pilots and navigators nodded in unison. Fair enough. They could hardly miss a whacking big place like North Africa. But the three wireless-operator air-gunners — WOP-AGs, in the idiom of the trade — were less attentive to such matters of direction and landfall, being more in harmony with wireless frequencies and the methods of clearing stoppages in their turret guns, should they get a crack at the enemy.

'Then you'll s-see the Western Desert road — a b-bloody long black strip — running p-parallel with the coast,' the mentor continued. 'So then you turn left and f-follow it until you come to the t-turnoff that leads you inland towards uk-uk-Cairo.' He swung his eyes around the semi-circle of sprog aircrew and raised his eyebrows in silent inquiry. 'Okay? It's a p-piece of uk-uk-cake.'

The skippers and navigators nodded again in unspoken assent. A piece of cake. Then an emboldened pilot ventured a request, a petty little emergency precaution, perhaps, and maybe too silly a thought to put to an officer of such high rank as a wing commander. 'Maps' sir? Do we get maps?'

'N-none here, sergeant. But you can't m-miss the coast and the Desert Road. Great l-long, black strip it is. Just f-follow that. Turn right at the junction. Then g-go along that until you c-come to LG26. That's where you'll l-land. Can't go wrong. It's a p-piece of cake. Got it?'

Gotcha.

'Well, get c-cracking as soon as you can before we g-get another raid. Otherwise I might k-keep you here. We're always looking for aircraft and crews.'

We had heard that a certain amount of pirating of Middle East-bound transit crews went on at Malta, as the state of aircraft serviceability and the fancy of the moment moved the autocratic powers on the island.

'Get yourselves off in formation and k-keep low on the d-deck, out of Jerry's radar. And k-keep a look-out for f-fighters, you air-g-gunners,' the wing commander advised.

Good thinking. An immediate start would suit all of us fine. So far, we had spent little more than twenty-four hours on Malta, but what we had seen, heard and felt around the place did not appeal. Perhaps, if we were compelled to remain longer, we too might develop stammers and stutters. Our beds during our brief stay in transit had been in a ward of the local poorhouse, by then requisitioned by the Air Force as the sergeants' dormitory. Our one night of tawdry recreation had been spent in pub-crawling down in Strada Stredda — the infamous 'Gut' — so our heads were thick and our stomachs were vile from peculiar and sinful conconctions.

We moved hastily towards our aircraft. My Blenheim — V6257 — was to lead the vic formation. My navigator was young Les Norman, a London clerk before he joined the RAF. Ces Dutton was my WOP-AG. He came from Chester and was something of a cricketer in his pre-war leisure pursuits. Frank Baum, another Londoner, was the pilot of my No 2 aircraft. He was called Snibbo for some obscure reason. His navigator was a young Welshman named Davies who, of course, could not be known by any other name than Taffy. Willy Williams, a diminutive and quiet young Englishman, was Snibbo's WOP-AG. Sergeant Stokes, an Australian who had flown his Blenheim in company with mine in our seven-and-a-half-hour flight from Gibraltar to Malta, tucked in as No 3 as we took off in the early morning air on 2 February 1942. And, as directed by the wing commander, we got down close to the wave tops 'twixt wind and water — the scant clearance of about twenty feet that we were to continue to fly, later, as daylight reconnaissance spy-planes over the Mediterranean.

As time passed and we drew further away from possible Luftwaffe attacks, we loosened formation and climbed a bit to ease our concentration. And after four or five hours we saw that the distant haze was really a wall of yellow dust rising from sea level to some thousands of feet.

Sand storm,' announced my young navigator, who had studied his Egyptology. 'They call it the *khamsin*.'

'I know what *I* call it,' I said, peering in vain for a landfall.

'Where's the bloody coastline?' Stokes called over the RT in his Aussie drawl. He, too, was concerned. 'How are we going to find that goddamn road in this shit?'

Snibbo Baum had silently disappeared in the dusty fog and the aircraft piloted by Stokes — who was still making coarse decibels over the RT — was but a ghostly shape seen intermittently through the gloom.

The desert seaboard, we had been told, was fairly low-lying. I called to the other pilots: 'We're on our own, now. I'm going down to see if I can find a break in this stuff. See you at LG26.'

No reply.

I eased the Blenheim lower. There came a break in the driving sand-mist and there, seen dimly and briefly, was the coast of North Africa. No sign of hills. Good. I brought the aircraft down through the dust; lower, lower yet, feeling a bit more confident now that a landfall had been established. And as we pressed on and crossed the coastline at about four hundred feet we saw, through the infrequent breaks in the sand storm, the black Western Desert road.

Man is not lost, as the motto printed on our navigation manual had assured us. I gave a yelp of delight, as passionate as Balboa, sighting the Pacific for the first time, may have uttered. And I turned to port.

Dutton, meantime, had discovered life in the arid wasteland below. 'A camel!' he cried. Verily, those humpy things he had seen in picture books really did exist.

But from my own little Hill in Darian I could see three-fifths of bugger-all. Finding the Western Desert road was one thing — in fact a very big thing — but keeping it in view within the murky maelstrom of dust and sand was another matter. We pressed on eastwards, losing and finding again that black ribbon of bitumen that was our only hope of visual navigation, until we at last came to the turn-off that led inland to Cairo. We then became all chirpy and were much inclined to make mirth of our earlier apprehensions. Flying, really, was great fun, was it not! I cackled through the intercom that time-mocked panacea for panic:

> 'When in danger, when in doubt,
> Run in circles, scream and shout.'

We had, by that time, been about six hours in the air since leaving Malta. God and the infinite sands of the desert alone knew where the aircraft of Baum and Stokes were. But surely we, at least, were now safe! LG26, here we come.

Although we eventually found the landing ground — some barely distinguishable khaki tents, a few heavy motor vehicles and the ubiquitious forty-four gallon petrol drums — we were also still very much in the murk of the sand storm. And as I made an exploratory, low-level pass over the field to try and locate a wind sock, a red Very light curved up ahead of me.

'What's that for?' Les Norman queried.

'They don't want us to land.'

'So where do we go?'

'We're going in here,' I said. 'I don't know where else I can go.'

'Jesus, Boss!' Dutton added his apprehensions, making serious concern unanimous within Blenheim V2657.

I brought the aircraft around in a low circuit pattern — I certainly did not attempt the prescribed one-thousand-feet drill as taught by my tutors — and dropped the wheels and the required amount of flap. Another red flare shot up. By this time the watchers on the ground must have been almost as worried as we were. I muttered a curse and continued to let the Blenheim descend on the final approach. My legs had begun to twitch and judder on the rudder pedals. What if I were heading for a tent, or a truck, or a stock-pile of petrol? My mouth was dry. Les Norman had the starboard side window open and from his jump-seat beside me he was helping to keep watch for the ground.

Ah! There ahead was a patch of hard-packed sand marked with oil and tyre burns — a runway of sorts. But by now it was slipping fast beneath our wheels.

'Up-up-up!' Norman yelled as a dune, no larger than a small mountain, suddenly appeared ahead of us. The wheels hit hard and there was a terrible wrenching and rending of metal as the Blenheim rose, hung in agony for a second or two, and then dived and crashed. The engines came to a sickening halt that would have made the engineers at the Bristol Aeroplane Company Ltd burst into tears. The three-bladed propellers gouged into the desert and were bent backwards in incongruous shapes. The port engine immediately burst into flames and the three of us, scared and bruised but not seriously injured, scrambled through the safety hatches and scurried from the blazing wreck.

The crash of Blenheim V6257.

A crash wagon emerged from the swirling sand storm and its fire crew set about saving as much of Blenheim V6257 as was within their powers. Nothing much of re-usable value came from their toils, but at least our personal gear was salvaged, along with the sealed aircrew report that I had been entrusted to deliver to whosoever might have the pleasure of being our commanding officer — always assuming that we should survive to join an operational squadron.

Later, with a fine disregard for honesty and service etiquette, and through the convenience of the lightly gummed flap of the envelope, I opened the document and was moderately surprised and not a little pleased to discover that our OTU mentors had considered us an above-average crew.

The RAF has — or then had — four categories into which aircrew members were slotted. Exceptional (which, as the name suggests, was reserved for the few), above-average, average and below-average. After reading my report I was to often wonder on the capabilities of the fellows labelled below-average. Still, the Allies won the war. Didn't they?

This gritty entry into Egypt somehow seemed to escape the customary rigmarole of official inquiry and documentation that usually accompanies even the slightest bump of fuselage or bend of aerofoil. The OC of LG26 even seemed a little sympathetic and told us, somewhat to my relief, that we had flown through the worst sand storm the Western Desert had known for two or three years and that the RAF had lost nine other aircraft that same day, all victims of Allah's wrath. So we were bathed and soothed and packed onto the tray of a service truck and sent off to Almaza, a reception depot near Cairo, to await our posting to a squadron.

And what of Baum and Stokes and their crews, you may well ask? Well, Snibbo's WOP-AG had been a diligent lad and, instead of listening to and joining in the repartee within his own aircraft (like one I could mention), he had been keeping a wireless watch for any official signals or directions. He had picked up the instructions that our flight of incoming Blenheims should fly to an airfield on the eastern side of the Nile delta, where there was comparative freedom from flying sand. So Snibbo Baum landed safely and it was, as he later told me, in the words of the wing commander at Malta, a piece of cake.

Stokes and his lads were not so fortunate. They found the Western Desert road without too much anxiety. But Stokes didn't like the look of the weather from there on, so he elected to set his Blenheim down on the bitumen highway and wait for clearer skies — and, presumably, to hell with any troops or Army convoys that might care to pass.

An aircraft, as all who are involved in aviation know, requires a reasonably long stretch of straight runway for landing or take-off. Hindered by swirling sand, Stokes was not to know that the section of

Western Desert road on which he chose to set down had a curve in it. So before his Blenheim had finished its landing run, and while it still had a considerable amount of speed, it came to the curve and, not being designed to turn like a motorcar, it hit the deep watertable on the side of the road and flipped onto its back.

Stokes and his navigator managed to get out with minor bruises. But the WOP-AG was hanging upside down from his safety harness and his companions couldn't release the clip. So they hacked him clear with the aircraft's emergency axe. But they didn't stand under him to cushion his fall and he landed on his head and suffered concussion.

We met up with Baum and his crew at Almaza. But after we left Malta I never again sighted Stokes and his companions. Their misadventures on (or rather, off) the Western Desert road had been recounted to me, along with the belly-laughing that usually accompanies tales told of other fellows' mishaps. We all joined in the laughter, of course, knowing that we, in turn, would be held up before our erstwhile training-unit companions as figures of fun when our escapades became public. Perhaps we laughed so that we didn't cry.

Baum and I, along with our merry men, had been at Almaza for about a week when it was discovered that we did, in fact, exist and that we were destined to become Maryland crews — the Glenn Martin light bomber then promising to come forward in sufficient quantity to replace the aged and obsolete Blenheim in the Western Desert.

No 223 Squadron would be our tutor unit — if ever it could be found in the big wilderness that was North Africa.

'It's up at Mersa Mutruh,' the movements officer at Almaza said, after much signalling and inquiry. 'Well, I think it is. That's where it was at last hearing.'

So we were given rail passes and two large wooden crates of rations, one for each crew. They contained hard biscuits, packs of sugar and cans of butter, jam, bully beef and condensed milk. There were also several packs of horrible 'V for Victory' cigarettes that were given free to the troops. Tea would be brewed at various stops along the way and we were told that we should push forward for our claims. Like everything that was considered so bloody easy in the eyes of those who didn't have to do it, it was a piece of cake.

We were driven to Cairo railway station. Or, more fittingly expressed, we were ordered to get aboard a *gharri* that was going into the city. A *gharri* in British military jargon was anything earthbound that moved on wheels. Bicycles, naturally, were exempt from this category. An Egyptian horse-drawn, four-wheeled passenger carriage was a *gharri*, from which all other vehicles obtained the appellation. Cars, lorries, buses, maybe machine-gun carriers — you name it. So we got to the train and were directed to some barbaric coaches that had surely been designed to carry even lower forms of life than Air Force 'other ranks'.

We travelled by night and by day, stopping often but resting little, until we got to Mersa Matruh, where we alighted and wandered piteously in a strange land in our search for 223 Squadron. The Air Force officers there shook their heads. They knew of no such unit. Were we sure we had got it right — 223 Squadron? Maybe the unit was back at Fuka and we had overshot it. There was a Maryland squadron there. Or maybe they were Blenheims? Or Wellingtons? Bombers they were, anyhow.

'That's right,' a young administration officer piped up. 'The squadron's at Fuka.'

Later, we reckoned he must have been one of those fellows in London who would invariably, and with utmost sincerity, point you in the wrong direction if you wanted to find Piccadilly or Leicester Square.

An Army *gharri* was returning to Alexandria and the driver was asked to drop us off at Fuka which, should you be of an inquiring nature was, and presumably still is, close to the coast and midway between Maaten Bagush and El Daba. We had, indeed, overshot Fuka by many a desert mile.

Well, when we six sergeants reported to the CO of the RAF unit at Fuka we found that it was 55 Squadron then in residence and that their aircraft were Blenheims. No, nobody in that squadron knew where 223 Squadron might be. 'But you lads had better stick around here while we get off a signal or two,' said the CO. He was a nice fellow and he made us very comfortable for the two days that we were there as his uninvited guests. And then the message came from Cairo that the unit we were looking for was on rest at Shandur, an aerodrome on the banks of the Suez Canal.

We were again sent on our travels, this time by a communications DC-3, and arrived at 223 Squadron on 15 February 1942. Nor did we feel, as that notable shipping line slogan put it, that getting there was half the fun.

Baum and I were given handling notes on the care and attention of the Glenn Martin Maryland and told that the following day we would be expected to get one airborne and, at our peril, get it back to earth in the same condition as it left the runway. As my total flying time at that stage amounted to a modest 224 hours and thirty minutes, I viewed my upcoming chore with some trepidation. The Maryland cockpit was a small fighter-type compartment and the machine was not designed for dual control. Furthermore, to add to the spice of adventure, all the instruments in the only available aircraft were calibrated in the metric system and all cockpit labels and warnings were in French, the aeroplane having been part of the quota originally intended for the pilots of France. It was a linguistic area in which I was completely lost.

However, a crisp young pilot officer whom we shall call Buckley (and at the same time apologise to all real Buckleys) showed me into the isolated navigator compartment in the nose of the aircraft, while he set things in motion and got us aloft. He called out his flying procedures over the intercom, put the machine into various attitudes of flight and we landed after about twenty minutes of airborne confusion.

'Okay, Sanders,' he said. 'Read up the gen on the Maryland for the rest of the morning and then you can go solo.'

My first handlings of the controls gave one of the airmen fitters the fright of his life. He was on the port wing root as I was about to taxi out for take-off. 'Take me along to the hangar as you go past,' he said, pointing to the building about two hundred yards along the apron.

Being used to the lengthy throttle travel of the Blenheim, I pushed the port and starboard levers forward and the aircraft, with much power on tap from but the slightest throttle advance, leaped forward and began a curve that promised to become a wicked ground-loop. I hauled back on the tits and advanced the other lever to correct the swing and the machine turned angrily in the other direction. The airman on the wing screamed, 'Throttle back! Throttle back!'

He got off smartly and decided to walk the short distance to the hangar. Meanwhile, nursing my fiery beast carefully, I got it to the end of the runway and with much apprehension and some clumsy skills, got the Maryland airborne.

I surveyed the dials that spoke of *essence* and *huile* and were numbered in metres — none of which had been mentioned in the handling notes of Marylands made for the English-speaking airmen

— and after exploring the characteristics of bank and climb and dive, I brought the machine into the circuit and began landing procedures. Pilot Officer Buckley was standing near the approach end of the runway and he sent off a red Very light to ward off my first attempt at landing a Maryland. I was coming in too high. However, after going around again I came in and set the aircraft down in a reasonable manner, sufficient for Buckley to permit me to complete a further five hours and forty-five minutes of solo flying before I was passed out as a qualified Maryland pilot, entrusted to carry my crew towards such hazards as the weather, the desert, the sea, the enemy and fate could fling at us. And, indeed, there were more than a few in the days to follow.

Snibbo Baum also passed the testing and emerged from 223 Squadron as a qualified Maryland pilot. It had been a ridiculously short course of two days, during which time I had had but twenty minutes of familiarity with the aircraft, sitting passively in the nose compartment. In seven solo flights I had completed exactly six hours. Presumably, Baum's experiences had been about the same. Anyway, we were both posted to 203 Squadron at Burg el Arab. And when we arrived on station we found that we were to continue to fly Blenheims. The squadron was still in the early stages of conversion to Marylands and the two or three of those aircraft that the unit possessed were reserved for flight commanders and senior pilots.

Baum and I, along with our crews, were required to attend lectures and sit a final exam on station, thereby becoming general reconnaissance crews and part of Coastal Command's broad overall plan that embraced aerial watch and attack over the Mediterranean.

It was my entry into operational flying with a maritime squadron. It was the beginning of a brief and impressive part of my wandering life. Wind and water were the elements of our airborne hours. Enemy fighters, sometimes flak, almost always cramps and tiredness and, too frequently, sand-scoured and weary engines were our foes. And now, as memory holds the door ajar, I can look back in time to the people and the places, the whys and the hows of its happening.

2

The Nestlings

In my memory, as though the scene was set but yesterday, it is again that early summer morning of Saturday, December 21 1940. Almost half a century has gone fleeting by, but the faces in that vision are ever-young and the excitements and apprehensions of the occasion remain vividly alive.

We are a heterogeneous lot as we spill out of the train onto the platform at Levin. In the dishabille that comes from sleeping in our clothes we shamble around in the morning air, scratching our unshaven chins and cautiously cupping hands over our throbbing vaccination wounds.

The night spent in the jolting, hard-seated day carriages has been wearisome. It had begun, on boarding the southbound express at Auckland, with an air of *élan* because we were at last on our way towards flying. But, after much roughhousing and little sleep, we had greeted the dawn short-tempered and rather ill. We are glad to stretch our legs and feel again the pavement under our feet.

The RNZAF non-commissioned officers who are waiting for us study their latest crop with contempt and disfavour. At the loading ramp of the railway station they have three open MT trucks ready to fill with raw material for the parade ground. Soon, for them, it will be harvest home. Slit-eyed and thin-mouthed, they gaze upon us. And they despise us.

But I am wrong. They merely affect malevolence. Secretly, as we are so soon to discover, they are glad to receive us. The war has been rumbling along for just over a year. Nine courses of embryo aircrew trainees have passed this way before us, and the sergeants and corporals of the ground training school have become adept at putting the thrall in his place. Their authority has been brief but omnipotent.

They are truculent with a martial power that is too new and strong a brew for their heads to hold. And within the stone crocks that serve as their hearts they are sadistically joyous to take us to their camp. For we are their daily bread, the stumbling, blundering, blushing butts of their bellowed orders and their sarcastic admonishments. We are their *raison d'être*.

We are herded into the MT vehicles when the sergeant has studied his freight manifest and is satisfied he has a full muster. Then, with the air and authority of a garbage contractor, he orders the driver of the first truck to move. 'Get cracking' is his precise command — which is a new phrase to most of us. It is one of those imported bits of service jargon which we are to hear so often over the years.

The RNZAF ground training station at Weraroa, Levin, enfolds us as we pass the satisfaction of the sentry at the gate. And soon we are rallying to hear our commanding officer spread the good word about our service future.

We stand like third-formers in the quadrangle, our multi-hued civilian clothing offensive to the eyes of the regular staffers of the station. We are bright-eyed and open-mouthed, pathetically eager to please our new mentor by laughing huh-huh-huh in unison at the jokes he has probably salvaged from the induction parade of Course No 1. Already we are mentally and physically recouped, and our irritabilities at the railway station are forgotten. God and the Commanding Officer are good; and all at Weraroa is wonderful.

Like a sage father eagle, the squadron leader proffers counsel and sounds his warnings to this assembly of nestling. He cannot and does not attempt to give us an in-depth dissertation on the cult or craft of flying. His concern of the place and the time is that we shall fill our soon-to-be-issued uniforms well, master the quick and the slow marches, slope and order arms, make our beds and fold our blankets tidily, fear God and keep the incidence of VD in the camp as low as possible.

Along the way, he tells us, there will also be much physical training, lectures on armaments, aircraft recognition, elementary airmanship and an introduction to meteorology. And, of course, there will be examinations on these subjects.

He does not tell us — this quiet, knowledgeable and kindly man —

that so very many of the fine young eaglets who are his audience this morning will not live to nest in the eyries of old age.

But not many of us are thinking upon such doleful consquences. None in the assembly is so naive as to imagine all of us gathered here on this bright day so close to Christmas will come safely through the combat that lies ahead. But surely all must feel as I do — that, whoever may fall, it is certain that I will survive! Each of us has been invested with a sublime confidence. Each of us is sure a certain star guides us on a safe path. Confidence, bright, blind confidence, is our benefaction. It is nature's goad for living; and in youth it burns with a strong white fire.

We are given numbers which, as time goes by, will become as important to the keepers of Air Force records as are our names. Mine is NZ405325, differing from Toby Webster's only by the transposition of the last two digits. The first two figures represent the year in which we have been inducted into the service. So henceforth we shall compare, either with envy or condescension, numeric relations with our fellow New Zealanders in divers air corridors of the world. The early volunteer is the sage, respected veteran.

Our blood samples are analysed and our religious denominations are recorded. The ciphers of this information are impressed, together with our service numbers, on fibre tablets, a pair of which are hung, for the duration of the war, from every neck. One is fireproof and one is rot-proof. So neither the fury of flame nor the corruption of the flesh nor the ravages of time, we are assured, shall expunge identification of our sorry bones.

We are divided into flights and squadrons. In a roster system I find I am, for a brief period of power and glory, flight commander of Flight 4B, No 1 Squadron. Toby Webster is with me, along with my namesake and tent-mate, Dudley Sanders. There is Wheeler, Walters, Williams, Mueller, Robinson and McGregor.

Dutch Stenborg, who became a ten-kill fighter ace before he was shot down and killed over France, is there. And there is Smeaton, Upton, Marks and likeable Terry Pepper.

Thorburn, O'Brien, Yates and Hunt; Mortimer, Lyall, Lomas and Kennedy; Hughes, Keesing and Jack Keys. We are so destined to march and study and roister together for a while, before the system eliminates some, and postings and death divide the others.

Now, as we steadily come to realize we are at last leading aircraftmen of the Air Force, we believe we walk taller. Certainly, we step out with an easy arrogance; and there stirs within us a growing wonder of the bright blue sky which we see now as something new and, henceforth, our own domain.

Guided by our still sketchy gleanings from meteorological lectures, we examine and mentally catalogue every cloud that intrudes the infinite dome of the heavens. The wispy mares'tails of cirrus show of winds high at 30,000 feet. And the anvil thunderheads of the cumulo-nimbus, we have been warned, will toss and shred a straying aircraft into a shower of crumpled aluminium pieces.

While our heads are in these clouds, our polished boots stamp the parade ground. The rifles we shoulder and the fixed targets we try to hit on the range have no place in our scheme of service. These performances are for the plebeian soldiery. We want to fly and we are impatient to get airborne. Some of us — quite a sizeable number, I suspect — have yet to break the bonds of earth as passengers in aeroplanes, let alone fly at the controls.

We have been told that some of us will not pass muster as pilots, that the great and inexorable law of averages shall decree that so many out of such-and-such a number will either be grounded for all time, or be re-mustered as observers or wireless operator-air gunners. Not one of us believes he will fail. Like death, the ignominy of aerial inadequacy is something that happens to the other fellow.

As yet, scarcely does the thought of personal conflict with the human enemy invade our minds. Our battles are, and will be for many months to come, with our own fears, our Government's aircraft and God's weather.

After some weeks of musketry, physical drill, lectures, disciplined sleeping habits, reduced alcohol intake and measured diet, we are lined up seven-deep on the grass playing field and photographed as one huge, smiling family.

In the comparatively short space of time spent at our initial training school, the thin have grown thicker, the pudgy have been whittled thinner and the tender have grown tougher. Our sergeants and corporals, snarling and barking us into our places so that we may grin and wait for the photographer's birdie to pop out, must secretly feel proud of their work. We have levelled well toward that uniformity that is the goal of the military disciplinarian.

Along with us, their pupils, some will keep the long, panoramic prints of such photographic gatherings; and over the next months — and for probably a year or so, if news reaches them — they will put an ink cross over the chest of one or another smiling image. The war will rumble on, and it will be hard to keep track of time and death. But the young, bold, eager faces will continue to smile back out of the yellowing, dusty prints.

Our time has come for us to leave Weraroa. We go back, on leave, to home and hearth and the pride of our respective families. We are fêted and paraded before all the relatives and friends our parents can alert for our homecomings. Our uniforms give us a status never before enjoyed; and the white flash in our forage caps, denoting we are chosen for aircrew training, adds lustre to the glamour.

Already, we feel, we must be gods in the chrysalis.

3

The Ecstasy and the Anguish

RNZAF Station Whenuapai in early 1941, let history show, was a wide grass airfield edged on the south-west side, as it is today, by two arc-roofed concrete hangars. Those structures, so recently then erected, smelled strongly of barely dry masonry, petrol and aircraft dope. They caught and magnified sound, as hangars always have and will, and tossed the echoes back and forth within their cavenous penetralia.

Mechanics and riggers worked on lame aircraft, and shouted and swore at each other through the workday hours; and in the hangars at night nested an amazingly large fleet of bright yellow Tiger Moth biplanes.

There were other buildings, naturally. Long dormitory blocks for the sheltering of airmen were there, along with mess halls for officers, sergeants and the lowly erks. And there were married officers' quarters, canteens, stores and, of course, the administration block between the two big hangars that we soon learned to call Bullshit Castle.

Toby Webster and I were among the many from Weraroa who were posted to Whenuapai, the home of No 4 Elementary Flying Training School, and for our introduction to the wonders of flight the course of pilot trainees was split into groups of about five for each instructor. For alphabetical reasons, Webster and I could not share the same teacher; so, along with Jack Keys, Mortimer, Richards and my namesake, Dudley Sanders, I was presented to Pilot Officer Doug Greig for his kindest attentions.

I had flown as a passenger in one or two open cockpit aircraft before I enlisted in the Air Force, my first flight being a ten-minute excursion of sheer ecstasy in a barnstorming DH-60G in 1930. The late Jim Hewitt was the pilot and the bumpy airstrip was a paddock in the Waingaro district. And the pre-flight excitement now, as my good tutor Doug Greig helped strap me into the yellow Tiger Moth, was the same as I had known before those earlier take-offs. Here too, conjuring back old and tingling thrills, was the characteristic aeroplane smell that was a coalescence of petrol, acetate, oil, leather, canvas, sweat, vomit and disinfectant.

On that first passenger flight in a service aircraft I was taken bouncing over the grass to hornet upwards to about six thousand feet. Pilot Officer Greig showed me rate-one turns and steep turns, encouraging me to follow his movements, exploringly, with my feet on the rudder bar and my hand on the stick — which latter device, my kindly guide demonstrated, was a quite sensitive thing and responsive in the extreme to human maulings. 'You hold it between thumb and your first two fingers,' he said. 'Just like you would a big, fat pencil.'

Doug Greig did not do anything particularly fancy or daring, because this was merely a flight to get me confidently familiar with the kindly Tiger Moth. But after a while, when he was satisfied I was not going to be sick all over the cockpit, he let me take the controls for a few minutes. We landed far too soon for my fancy and my eager companions, impatiently awaiting their turns bug-eyed with antici-pation, begged my opinions of flight.

I told them it was bloody marvellous.

The dormitory blocks were particularly noisy that night. Every one of the pupil pilots, having been carried aloft on a beautifully calm February day, was certain he had been born to fly. Patient instructors had put the cheery little aeroplanes through the gentlest of manoeuvres, so that the business of piloting was just too goddamn easy. There was horseplay with the fire extinguishers and much shouting and splashing in the shower cubicles until, one by one, the tired and happy fellows settled down and sought quiet corners. Out came the pens and the writing compendiums that mothers and sisters and sweethearts had given them as goads to correspondence; and they wrote home with a little extra pride, and perhaps an exaggeration or two, on the pages: '. . . And coming back to base, I flew the aeroplane *myself.*'

The days that followed saw us labouring hard for the proficiency that would allow us to fly solo. We were shown how to extricate our gyrating machines from tight spins and how to hold the nose of the aeroplane around the horizon in steep turns.

'Bank and rudder — bank and rudder, as we go into the turn,' chanted Pilot Officer Greig. 'And then we tighten it up — tighten it up. And as we increase the rate of turn, so the rudder becomes the elevator — and the elevators become the rudder.'

How?

On the ground again, Doug Greig patiently showed us, with the aid of a model aircraft mounted on a pedestal, how those bewildering aerodynamics worked.

We went, as thrilled and tremulous passengers, through the aerobatics of the loop, praying that our webbing safety straps would hold us as we hung upside-down at the top of the arc, watching petrol piddling out in a spray from the simple gauge above the mainplane.

And here we go again — down, down, down at the exhilarating rate of 130 mph, with the wind screaming through the flying wires. Then the pull-out — and the full-powered zoom up, up, up until the engine is fighting and faltering against the fundamental law of gravity. And the stick is pulled back; and over we go, the passenger holding hard to anything fixed and solid within his cockpit, the pilot throwing his head back and looking from the tops of his eyes to find the horizon; and seeing the landscape, six thousand feet below, rush into view.

Circuits and bumps. We had them, over and over again. Sometimes we felt we had the wretched landings tamed and that we would be off solo in record time. But next time around we would come in with a mighty bounce that would, literally, bring us down to earth with a jolt. And five, six, seven and eight hours of dual flying would be entered in our log-books.

Getting off on our first solo flight became a matter of fierce competition and pride of achievement. I was off on my own after a little more than nine hours of dual instruction, which was somewhere around the average mark. Flying an aircraft solo for the first time is an event that merits a special place in a pilot's record of distance run. It is a peculiarly personal triumph for him to treasure and cling to, in heartening recall, when the poor seasons follow. It is something of creativity made manifest. It is something he has done that is in absolute defiance of nature, and the triumph can never ever be taken from him.

Some may describe certain pilots as 'natural flyers' whose inheritance is the wind and the nimbus. But this cannot be so. So far as records and theories show, man was never descended from winged creature. Theologians will say that he was created as intact as he walks today; and evolutionists may argue that he had his beginnings in some protoplasmic ooze washed up on some shore by the sea.

Ergo, man may conceivably be a natural runner or climber; or yet a picker of forbidden fruit. Or perhaps, if imagination would allow, he could be a natural swimmer. But a flyer? No. He will continue to battle his airborne way against nature in defiance of gravity. Science, studied skills, determination, a little bit of stupidity and a lot of luck will keep him aloft.

My chance to fly solo came about quite unexpectedly. I had bungled one or two dual landings and was feeling frustrated and disappointed, so I was surprised when my instructor stopped taxying the machine, throttled back the engine and climbed out of his front cockpit with a few grunts and hefted his parachute onto the grass. He did not say a word until he had removed his control column and neatly stowed his safety straps. Then he said: 'Okay, you're off. Just give her a couple of circuits — and remember what I've told you.'

I taxied downwind for take-off, weaving the prescribed path the Tiger Moth pilot must traverse so that he does not tangle propellers or chew the tail off another aeroplane that might be obscured by his machine's raised nose. I turned cross-wind and looked for traffic before checking my tail trim and moving the aircraft into wind. Then, pushing the throttle steadily forward, I concentrated on keeping the machine straight as I bounced over the grass; the tail came up and soon I was airborne.

As the little Tiger Moth hummed and wallowed its way upward I sang joyously. Checking my direction and my airspeed, I continued my climb to the prescribed eight hundred feet before beginning my first turn of the circuit. As Whenuapai and Hobsonville were so close that our circuit patterns, in certain circumstances, overlapped, we were flying right-hand exercises on this day. I turned west, carefully watching bank and rudder, and keeping the nose of the machine up. I was at one thousand feet and it was time to fly the downwind leg. Watching my height, my course and the airfield slipping by below on my right, I waited for the down wind end of the grass runway to come into view from under the trailing edge of the starboard wing. And then it was time to turn across-wind.

I can fly, I realised with pride and wonder and joy. Now, let me see how I can land this aeroplane! Now is the time to turn into wind on the final approach towards the field. I come down, down, down, with power cut back and the engine making gentle pop-pop-pop noises, and the two-bladed wooden propeller flopping around almost lazily. I have been told to listen to the wind in the rigging wires. If they send forth a subtle sibilation my speed of descent is fine. If they are silent, I had better prepare for a stall. But I have judged my glide-path well enough, and I can see I will safely clear the new earthworks bounding the threshold of the field. I concentrate on keeping the little aeroplane dead into wind and prepare to level off for flare-out. I am down — bump-bump-bump. Wheels and tail-skid have hit the ground together in an approved three-point landing and the Moth runs free-wheeling over the grass to a standstill.

I am gasping with excitement and triumph. My achievement, won against air and gravity, machinery and myself, has been something akin to the passing of a pagan tyro warrior's initiation into a select brotherhood. I taxi back, exultant, and again head into wind. Once more I open the throttle and climb towards the sky.

The days of lectures, physical training, rifle range practice and parade ground drill interspersed the hours we spent in the air. We developed our awakening aerial skills in practising precautionary landings, forced landings, taking off out of wind, aerobatics and, under the watchful and twittery guidance of our instructors, instrument take-offs.

Cloistered in the cockpit by a gadget called 'the hood', and denied the sight of anything except the instrument panel and the simple furniture around him, the pupil pilot fought with controls and his insistent instincts to keep the aircraft travelling straight while coaxing it into the air. The instructor, able to see the hazards that lay in the wayward paths the pupil might choose to weave, suffered in morale much more than the groping fledgeling. And a hefty kick on the dual-controlled rudder bar, or an emphatic pull back on the throttle when take-off was beyond recovery, let the novice know that he had strayed from the very straight and narrow pathway that is instrument flying.

From time to time, senior flying instructors from RNZAF Station Hobsonville — the instructors of our instructors — would call on No 4 EFTS and take random samplings of pupil pilots for check flights. The purpose, presumably, was to find out how our young instructors were imparting all the good work they had learned at Hobsonville.

My namesake, Dudley Sanders, was one of the Whenuapai pupil pilots chosen for one of those snap checks. But that day was a bad one for Dudley — and it was not a good one for me, either. Unfortunately, my namesake had a most unreliable stomach and had, on one or two earlier occasions, been physically sick while flying. And, to cap it, his check flight was not one of his happier exercises.

Soon after Dudley's command performance, I was told that I would have to have a flight commander's check flight. To me, who had managed to get around the sky without giving either myself or my instructor any hang-ups, this came as a most disconcerting surprise. A flight commander's checks, as all of us knew, was the end of the road for a pupil pilot. It was a formality that took the burden of responsibility from the shoulders of an instructor.

Instead of his having to say: 'Okay, Perkins, you're wiped out — finished,' he could mumble: 'Um. . . er. . . Perkins, I think maybe we'll give you a flight commander's test, just to double-check on how you're shaping up.'

And all the luckless Perkinses who heard those melancholy words would feel a bit sick in the stomach. And some would weep with chagrin. For how, after all the brave words they had spoken of eagles and aerial conquest, would they be able to face their families and their sweethearts?

Some, after the affront to their pride had settled, would quietly thank their God for his kindly intervention. 'I was taken off flying,' they could always say, and in their hearts they could console themselves: 'I didn't quit. Oh, my Lord God, but I wanted to. But I didn't. I didn't quit.' And they found a quiet peace.

I found no peace, whatsoever, in the knowledge that I was to be so tested. In a high old fizz of bewilderment, anger and apprehension, I climbed into the cockpit behind my flight commander, Flight Lieutenant Tony Firth. Alert for the flying discrepancies that had been reported to him he found, first, that I was gunning the throttle too fast on take-off. He found, too, that the nose of the aircraft fell below the horizon on one of my steep turns. And one of my cross-wind landings was not up to standard.

We landed, and the touch-down was not too bad, at that. Walking along the concrete strip in front of the hangar, the master said to the expectant apprentice: 'I really don't know, Sanders. I don't know. Er. . . have you ever considered being a navigator?' The man was clearly perplexed, but he had a report that begged his concurrence. Did he support a fellow officer's judgement — or did he agree that this confused trainee had shaped up to an average standard of airmanship?

Had I ever considered being a navigator? Hell, I had initially enlisted as a wireless operator-air gunner, been promoted in my application papers to the status of observer (or navigator), and had been provisionally accepted by the selection committee as a pilot-under-training. Yes, of course I had *considered* being a navigator, the same as I had considered, at various stages of my childhood, being a fireman, an engine driver and a speedway star.

But I had become determined that I would be an Air Force pilot. And that is what I told Flight Lieutenant Tony Firth.

I was told to go away and await further advice.

I was thoroughly confused and horribly dejected; however, the fact that Toby Webster had been held back for a couple more weeks of further training was, at least, some small compensation and a salve for my bruised pride.

The departure of Number 10 Course from Whenuapai was now imminent and the rest of the gang, on the very eve of being posted to their next stages of flying instruction, were rushing in all directions as they prepared themselves in their 'number one' uniforms ready to catch the MT transports that would take them to the Auckland railway station. Toby and I decided that we would take a leave pass and cut loose in the city to lose our woes.

We were shaving in the ablution block when one of our fellows came bounding in with the word that I was wanted at the Station Commander's office. 'There's been a mistake,' he said, 'and you're coming with us, after all!'

I arrived at Bullshit Castle breathless and grinning widely. I was ushered into the Station Master's office by an orderly and I snapped to attention, saluted and blurted out the most stupid utterance that any airman can say to an officer: 'Sir. . . I understand there's been a mistake, Sir!'

The boss shook his head soberly, although the other three officers, poring over trainee-pilots' personal documents, grinned. 'No, there's been no mistake, Sanders. But we've decided to send you on.'

He went on at some length about his wish that I should do my best wherever I went in my service career and not letting his station down. And then he charged me with the toughest task I had yet to face in the Air Force up to that time. He handed me a sealed envelope and said: 'When you get to the Auckland railway station, will you please hand this to LAC Sanders — the other Sanders — and ask him to report back to Whenuapai as soon as possible.'

I did not need the facts displayed in chapter and verse to know, now, that Dudley had been the intended one for the flight commander's test and that I, in error, had been called to fly the exercise. Presumably, as I had not done anything extraordinarily wrong on the test, my examiner had delved deeper into the simple mysteries of bureaucracy and had found the foul-up.

I left the station administration block now firmly convinced the old castle was aptly named. I went back to our billet, said my farewell to Toby Webster, and was soon on my way to RNZAF Station Ohakea, and No 3 IFTS.

4

Per Ardua Ad Terra Firma

If you live long enough in your flying career you will some day have a crash or a prang. A crash, as the very sound of the name suggests, is an awful breaking and rending of metal or, should you be flying a vintage service job or a flying club machine, a shattering of wood and much ripping of fabric. In this area of disaster, fire is often in attendance. And so is death.

A prang, which rhymes with 'twang', is usually associated with less dramatic damage to the aeroplane or the pilot's nervous system. It can run the scale of calamity all the way from a bent wing-tip up to or down to a crumpled undercarriage and an engine that has been telescoped backwards into the driver's lap.

Survivors of a crash rub their charm beads and vow to go to church more often. Those emerging from a prang inevitably feel humiliation, for the expense of aircraft repairs and replacement can be extraordinarily high, and the machine's owner or his representatives can get very cross.

My first prang in one of His Majesty King George VI's aircraft came, literally, out of the blue, when I was attempting my third or fourth solo landing in an Airspeed Oxford at No 3 Intermediate Flying School, RNZAF Ohakea. It was the first of five hard collisions with the ground that I was to experience during my eight years of Air Force flying. The desert sand and the unruly elements played a major part in two of the accidents, an aircraft's perfidy and its own fuel system caused one, enemy action caused another and the first, soon to be related, was the outcome of sheer ignorance on my part.

All could have brought serious hurt to the occupants of the machines, but the luck that often travels with aircrew was, in every case, smiling — if not sardonically laughing fit to wet itself.

The scene comes vividly to mind as I turn back the pages to the days when Ohakea was a grass airfield and its *raison d'être* was a training arena for the shaping of raw learner-pilots into sergeants and pilot officers qualified to wear the flying brevet we called our wings.

The year of 1941 is still young and it is high summer. And we who have arrived from our initial triumphs and our obediences of the laws of lift, gravity, thrust and drag, have become somewhat sobered from our early intoxications with elementary flight. Although we will continue at times to get heady with the strong wine of aerial adventure, we now raise the cup with more caution as we drink to our youthful, everlasting powers. For we have found, too close at hand, that life is by no means abiding and that fortune is fallible. The facts have been made manifest, right here within our circle of companions.

Little Tiny Trainor fell to his death in an Auckland suburb, trapped within his Tiger Moth when the wings collapsed and folded over his cockpit while he was performing acrobatics for the entertainment of his family and friends below. Clousten cartwheeled his aeroplane on the sandhills of Muriwai Beach, but managed to survive that escapade with injuries which hospitalized him for weeks. Tom Kirk flew his Airspeed Oxford into the hills beyond Palmerston North while night flying. Supposedly, he had committed the cardinal sin of navigation. By setting his compass 'red on black' instead of 'red on red' he had flown a reciprocal course into the dark bush heights of the Ruahine Ranges.

Toby Webster and I were among the many mourners at his burial service at St Andrew's Church in Epsom, Auckland. And, because I was moist eyed, Toby tried to brace me. 'We'll see many more of our mates go like this, before the war is over.' He tolled his own knell.

Another Airspeed Oxford, taking off from a South Island airfield with an overnight coating of ice on its wings, was a victim of its own inability to overcome local stalling at the wing roots. Friend Peter McNab managed to survive, but the pilot died. The machine had crashed far from our part of the country, but the couriers of doom and despondency who had relayed the news added bits and pieces to the story of disaster, seeking to prove that this two-engined monoplane trainer to which we were now committed was, in solemn fact, Yellow Death with a High Wing Loading.

But the Oxford, we are persuaded by our instructors, is, like any other tried and proven aeroplane, just a machine demanding its due respect. Any contraption of metal, plywood and wire that leaves the ground is at once capable of giving hurt. Coaxing it into the air is relatively simple, but getting it and, importantly, yourself back softly to earth is the big thing we should strive for. Everything that goes up must come down; and I am therefore of the opinion that the Air Force motto, instead of goading us with *Per Ardua Ad Astra* should instead applaud us with *Per Ardua Ad Terra Firma*. Through effort and adversity to the ground is the summary of all man-made flight.

Airspeed Oxford of the RNZAF.

For all our ignorant apprehensions of its reputed vices, the Oxford has been responsible for the training of thousands of Air Force pilots and the accident level has been kept relatively low. Around its shapely fuselage and within its compact cockpit, the enthusiasts claim, every prospect pleases and only man (meaning, of course, the pupil) is vile. But I am not so sure of this as I stoop through the aeroplane's doorway on the port quarter and hunch my way forward. I am not happy with the smell of the beast. It has a pungent, uncharitable stench quite different from the cheery, outdoors tang of the little

DH-82. And I am to discover, as time rolls by, that every breed of aircraft has its own characteristic aroma, perfume or stink — every whiff evocative of past aeronautical pleasure or pain.

To my eyes, wide with wonder and ignorance, the cockpit is an instrument-maker's showroom and I am sure I cannot digest the silent clamourings of advice and warning that the complexity of dials and knobs will throw at me. My instructor at No 3 IFTS is Pilot Officer Tony Harris. He encourages me into the left seat and goes through his tutorial patter as we prepare for starting.

We have power in both engines. We jolt our taxying way downwind across the grass to the take-off end of the field, where Harris runs up each engine and takes a final check against magneto drop. The green Aldis signal from the control tower tells us the runway strip is clear for us. Harris does his cockpit check aloud for my benefit, chanting the mnemonic: 'T-M-P-F-F — trim, mixure, propeller, fuel, flaps.' He goes through the motions of touch and adjust. He explains: 'The propeller of the Oxford is fixed-pitch, but we include its mention in our cockpit drill. Someday you'll be flying variable-pitch aircraft and you won't want to forget your fine-pitch drill for take-off.'

We turn into wind and begin to roll forward. My instructor, as his dual controls, opens the throttles slowly, checking a slight swing to the right as we gain speed. The Oxford's tail comes up and we are tooling across the grass at 60-65 mph. Harris lifts the machine off, holds it low for the speed to build, and then begins to climb the aeroplane at about 90 mph. He lets this increase to a rate of 110 mph as we continue upwards to six thousand feet.

My tutor puts the aircraft through some of its general paces, allowing me to get the feel of aileron, elevator and rudder controls. I am awed and thrilled to realize that I am at the controls of this two-engined airborne monster. We do medium turns and try a steep turn or two. We glide down towards a small cloud, visualizing it as an airfield, and we carefully watch the airspeed indicator and the altimeter as though this is a real landing approach. We practise stalls and how to regain safe flying speed, and we practise overshoots, so tha: I know how to raise the undercarriage and take up the degrees of flap with discretion.

My familiarization flight in the Oxford satisfactorily completed, Harris now concentrates on giving me a series of circuits and landings. And, now convinced that I have my procedures tamed, he prepares to leave me in sole charge.

'Now remember what I have told you,' he cautions as he vacates his right-hand seat. 'Climb straight up to eight hundred feet before you turn left on your cross-wind leg. Then, still climbing, you reach one thousand feet and you turn on to the down-wind leg.'

He is making curving motions with his right hand, impressing on me that this plane of flesh represents our aeroplane in a graceful rate-one bank to port.

'You then go down-wind until the down-wind end of the airfield comes into view from the trailing edge of your wing. Got it?'

I nod. I say, 'Yessir.'

'So you've dropped your undercarriage and you've selected thirty degrees of flap', he continues. 'You've turned across wind now, and you are manoeuvring your aircraft for the final approach, dropping off height and watching your airspeed. You don't want to be doing any S-turns, so you turn into wind early, coming down, down — mixture rich, flaps fully down, watching your height and the wind sock and the smoke-pot in the middle of the airfield.'

He pauses and points so that I can see, through the windscreen, the swirl of grey smoke that emanates from a grass-level source amidfield. 'The wind's a wee bit tricky. Seems to be on the change. So take it steady, eh!'

The first two or three solo landings were fine. I managed my flare-outs well enough to meet the grass without causing Tony Harris too many heart palpitations, as I remember. But disaster struck me on, I think, my fourth solo attempt. I came rumbling down towards the grass airfield and made ready to flare out and hold the Oxford ready for touch-down. But by this time the wind had increased and the air was rather boisterous. The left wing dropped, one wheel hit the ground hard and the aircraft ballooned high. Too ignorant to gun the throttles and take the machine around the circuit again, I tried to ride out the bounce without power. The Oxford stalled and came down heavily again on the left wheel, breaking off the oleo leg and nosing its snout into the turf. The other undercarriage leg was torn off and the two wooden propellers were splintered. The aeroplane lay panting on its belly, wisps of smoke rising from its so-suddenly interrupted engines, and the klaxon horn, which was intended to alert the pilot that his undercarriage had not been selected in the down position should the engine revolutions reach a slow beat, was blaring its heart out in bewilderment. There was fractured plywood and broken Perspex littered over a wide area.

The field became alive with movement. The OC Flying came motoring in the most handy vehicle he could commandeer; and he was followed by the ambulance and the fire wagon — whose crew, I fancy, were more intent on recovering the shards of Perspex which, in the fullness of time, they would fashion into paper-knives and brooches to give to girlfriends or sell at extravagant prices.

I was relatively uninjured, everything considered. I was sent to the station medical officer for an official check and then I returned to the flight office, humiliated and feeling as outcast as a pariah, to write a detailed report of my misadventures. Later, I was taken in a check flight by a senior instructor. He was an understanding chap who had, in his younger days and before my time in that district, worked on the same sheep station where I had been the head shepherd. We found much in common and soon established a rapport; and, after several landings, I was considered capable of taking an Oxford into the air again and, importantly, getting it and myself back to earth.

It gives me some comfort to know, when I look through my log-books, that all my flying assessments give me above-average ratings so, despite the list of breakages debited against me over the ensuing years, my superiors undoubtedly found something of value in my airmanship.

After the more elementary flying exercises were completed in the daytime schedule, we were introduced to night flying. I found that I had a particular affinity for this work and loved being part of it — of taxying my machine out through the darkness to pause at heaven's gate; to see, in those early days, the avenue of flickering goose-neck flares that showed my pathway to the stars; to move the throttles forward and feel the power of engines, and know the thrill of lifting the aircraft into the night to cruise above the earthly lights, a minion of the moon, among a million other planets.

By cautiously observing the rule book I emerged through a series of aerial exercises and theoretical tests to No 3 Advanced Training School, another department of Ohakea Station. Here we were given the earnest treatment in the skills of air-to-air gunnery, firing a Vickers gun from the dorsal turret of the Oxford at a deceptively evasive canvas drogue target towed by one of our companion's aircraft.

We practised both high- and low-level bombing on the lupin-covered range in the sandhills, and we sweated over formation flying and practical navigation exercises. And so, in time, we were considered ready to sit the examination that, if conquered, would gain us our prized wings.

It is of some interest to know that all of Course 10C passed the tests. Some of us were assisted by native cunning and deceit more than by scholastic competence. We had access to the classrooms before the various papers were set in front of us, and it was not unknown for candidates to slip in beforehand and scribe onto the desks such basic formulae that might assist in their answers. Some missed their selected seats in the scramble when the doors were opened and great was their frustration and anger. Others, who had their crib-cards tucked inside cigarette packets, were the more sophisticated and the more fortunate cheaters.

The earning of wings, or the flying brevet, was acclaimed on some Air Force stations, particularly in Canada, as an occasion of considerable pomp and ceremony, when the hard-won emblem was personally pinned onto the swelled chest of the graduate by his commanding officer, the proud parents among the invited guests viewing the parade through misty eyes. But at Ohakea, in June 1941, we were advised by a notice on the board in our dormitory block that the pupil-pilots listed thereunder were entitled to collect, from the quartermaster's store, ' Flying Badges, two — Pilots for the use of '. So we rushed to the barn-like place that smelt of camphor, breasted the counter, and filled in our requisition forms in triplicate.

Within the half-hour each joyful, and now fully accredited, pilot had sewn the embroidered symbols onto his two uniform tunics, leaving, of course, sufficient space between badge and the top of the pocket for any decoration ribbons that might later come his way.

It was academic that I would not gain a commission along with my passing the wings examination. I had broken a valuable aeroplane and, to add to my disgracing the service thus, I had earlier got myself involved in a physical altercation with one or two army fellows in the main street of Palmerston North one night. I had, for too many days thereafter, wandered around the station and the sky with two horribly blackened eyes inadequately shaded by dark glasses. Officers and gentlemen do not brawl. In theory they comport themselves with dignity and leave the milling and mixing of fisticuffs to that broad body of the armed services known as 'other ranks'.

Seven of our course members became acting pilot officers and they sat, solemn and pious, in the front row while we nine sergeant-pilots stood behind them as we posed for the official passing-out photograph.

And soon after that we received our posting instructions that would take us a step nearer the war front.

I see again, with crystal clarity, those days immediately following the winning of our wings. Now on final leave, we walk the streets of our home towns with mixed emotions. We are excited and perhaps a little apprehensive, for most of us are soon to be sailing overseas. But if there is no self-pride in our accomplishments, we are not human, for we know that we have passed stringent physical tests, have pitted our mental skills and our cunning wits against carefully prepared classroom examinations and have, above all, met some of the challenges and adversity in the air.

We are fit and alert young men who have been carefully selected for the further cultivation of those qualities, and have been painstakingly instructed in the rudimentary techniques that lead towards aerial warfare. We are now at the stage where we must go forward to learn more about pitting ourselves against other fit and alert young men of other lands, the vagaries of aerofoils and petrol engines, and the wrath of the winds and the nimbus.

We are, in the main, celibate young men. Our loins hold the seeds of untold generations of future fit and alert young men and women. Humanity — the procreation of the species — has need of just such as we can give. But the very virility that urges us to grow and mate and father a nation is, alas, the same strength that is demanded of us to go forth and destroy. So we press forward inexorably, as inevitably as germ battles against germ, and as militant as any battalion of ants on the rampage. Our Labour politicians in governmental power — some who preached pacificism in the Great War and were, indeed, gaoled for their refusal to fight — now send us overseas to meet the enemy, and there is much patriotic fervour in their speeches. And God, who has given us our higher powers of reason, but has left us with our blind, animal urges of survival and conquest, must look down on our confusion and grin.

I spend my days at home with my Mother. I am impatient to be on my way to Britain. But Mother, a widow for many a lonely year, hopes forlornly that peace will be declared before my ship sails. Webster has, long before, sailed for Canada and is being trained to fly in Harvard aeroplanes. I call on his mother and I am instructed to always keep an eye on the lad — should we (as she is so certain) meet up 'over there'.

Tom Kirk has gone — for all time. I call on his mother, too. She gives me some of his Air Force shirts, his dressing gown and his St George Rowing Club blazer. She is fiercely proud of her two sons who volunteered to go to war. Her flying boy lies in a new grave in St Andrew's churchyard Epsom. The other is a lieutenant in the New Zealand Army. Soon she is to learn that she has lost both of her children.

★   ★   ★

Late in July 1941 we get our message in the mail and we are shepherded aboard the liner *Dominion Monarch* which, now impressed to serve as a troopship, has arrived in Auckland with a noisy contingent of Australian airmen already in occupation. My cabin mates are Jack Keys, Roper McCarthy and an ex-policeman, also a McCarthy, who is soon dubbed Slapsie. We buy a second-hand portable gramophone and a pile of records, and shake down within our new home — a four-berth cabin amidships. And from that day onwards, Cole Porter's *Begin the Beguine* is to become forever associated with those nights and days as we sail towards Britain.

Our first port of call since leaving Auckland is Curaçao. Our ship needs fuel oil. One of the Aussie airmen, whose declared intention is to lay at least one woman in every port of call, gets the Caribbean instalment of his wide-ranging wish from a mercenary lady who beckons him from a balcony. And he discovers, some days later, that he is host to a souvenir that comes gratis with the union.

From Curaçoa we move northwards to the convoy assembly point of Halifax, Nova Scotia, where we spend a week of shore leave. I meet up again with Toby Webster, Dave Waters, Dutch Stenborg, Robbie Robinson and many others of the gang from our Weraroa and Whenuapai days, and the licensed liquor houses in the town do big business.

The Canadian-trained New Zealanders have finished their schooling in this part of the world and are in the Halifax transit camp awaiting passage to Britain. But although we take on a large detachment of airmen, Webster and his crowd are not included. We leave the port in convoy on a bleak and fog-grey day for the last stage of our journey across the U-boat-menaced waters of the Atlantic.

It is another day of fog and a perishing north wind's whipping when we make our landfall. I see this rock looming out of the mist of early morning; yet, strangely, I seem to know that I come here not as a stranger. It is somewhere near the year 5000 BC. Or is the era younger yet? Again, I sense, I am an early tribesman of the Archaic White paddling stubbornly against the tide, stretching my boundaries, forcing my way through evolution and history towards a new homeland. In my many, many lives I have come this way before and instinct, insistent and undeniable, has made clear the seaways, the shoals and the channels. Method has resolved itself across the ages, so that my primitive coracle of hide-leather and rough woodland timber is now a high-riding iron craft. And my fellow venturers on this journey are many.

My lineage, I feel, is as ancient as these islands. I am homeward bound — and almost there.

At Liverpool we are bundled into oversized Hornby trains and sent peeping and rattling southwards to Bournemouth, which is a city blue with the uniforms of newly-arrived airmen. For here is one of the Royal Air Force's big reception depots.

Webster, Waters, Stenborg and all their rowdy companions arrive while we are still sightseeing and kicking our heels with impatience to become airborne. They have come from Halifax by way of Iceland and they regale us with amazing tales of amorous adventures enjoyed along the way.

We soon get our postings to our respective operational training units, where we are to learn to fly front-line operational aircraft. Keys, Papps, Wacher, Parker, Finlayson and I are ordered to entrain for Bicester, Oxfordshire, where we are to plumb the rather simple mysteries of the Blenheim light bomber. Stenborg, destined to train on fighter aircraft, is ever the comedian. Bidding us farewell, he assures us, by the law of averages and the current rate of destruction, no Blenheim pilot will survive the war. Notwithstanding, he urges, we are to have fun before our imminent demise catches up with us.

Alas, Dutch Stenborg dies before any of us, falling to enemy fire over France after he has notched up ten kills as a Spitfire ace.

Webster is posted to an airfield somewhere in the Midlands where he will learn to fly Wellington bombers. We are destined to meet again on a couple of occasions in London, until . . .

Dave Waters, Robbie Robinson and the others? They go their many ways and most will be lost trails. Only by chance will a familiar face appear at the New Zealand Forces Club in the Strand, or perchance on some visited airfield. Or a known name may appear in the gazetted casualty lists that are now burgeoning with bereavement.

5

Bicester and its Blenheims

Late in 1978 my wife and I revisited Britain on our second return since we departed that land for New Zealand in 1945. With a bit more time to spend than I had on our earlier trip in 1970, I had the urge to travel to Bicester and see again the old town, and to gaze once more on the Air Force station where we six New Zealand sergeant-pilots had learned to fly the faithful Blenheim, back in 1941.

We alighted from the train at Bicester station to survey a scene completely different from the picture of rural quietude I had cosseted in my memory for close to forty years. All around were houses of amber brick and terracotta tile. Seemingly hundreds upon hundreds of them. A young city had grown since I was last here.

'We'll head for the Fox Inn,' I said. 'That's where we used to gather and knock back our pints in the evening. That's where we were on 7 December 1941', I said, tying time and place to history, 'when we heard, on the pub's wireless, Roosevelt announce that Japan had attacked Pearl Harbor — the "day of gross infamy".'

'So how do we get there?' Dorothy asked. 'It can't be far, can it?'

I looked for recognizable landmarks, but couldn't find anything that would prompt recall. 'I suppose we walk.' And we set forth. But I hadn't reckoned on my old enemy, arthritis, spiking my guns. Suddenly, my aching back and hips were letting me know that an exploratory stroll of any distance would be quite out of the question. So we hailed a nearby taxi and within two minutes we were at the Fox Inn.

We entered the pump room, its details and decor as yet but vaguely remembered. As Dorothy nibbled on her ploughman's lunch and sipped her gin-and-tonic, I wandered around, inspecting the pictures on the walls. And suddenly I came upon something wondrous to behold! There, framed and glazed, was the whimsical black-and-white illuminated address that I had drawn in Indian ink and dedicated to 'Mine Host, Ed Spencer, of the Fox Inn, Bicester' precisely thirty-seven years earlier. Affixed was a group snapshot of we six New Zealand sergeant-pilots snugged in our Irvin jackets; and underneath it we had signed our names — Alan Parker, Motueka; Jack Keys, Ellerslie; Pete Finlayson, Morrinsville; Colin Papps, Wanganui; Dave Wacher, Dunedin; Jim Sanders, Epsom, Auckland.

The text, beneath a badge of a kiwi riding a bomb, read:

> 'In recognition of your sterling hospitality, your fine ale, generous cigarettes and the cheerful, musical atmosphere of your house, we the undersigned NZ sergeant-pilots of Course (?), No 13 OTU, RAF Bicester, do hereby proclaim the Fox Inn as the ace No 1 NZ House of Bicester, and we trust our following fellow countrymen derive as much pleasure from their visits to this rendezvous as we all have.'

Fascinated, emotionally moved, I approached the woman serving drinks behind the bar. I waved a hand towards the framed eulogy hanging on the wall: 'I'm one of those New Zealand fellows in that photograph,' I said. 'In fact, I'm the one who designed the thing.'

She raised her eyes from filling a tankard and smiled: 'Oh yes!' And then, quite casually, she queried: 'You'd be the one standing at the right of the photograph, would you?'

'That's me.'

'We've seen a lot of interest in that picture,' she said. 'Lots of New Zealanders — and others, too — have looked at it, over the years.' She continued: 'Colin Papps was here a couple of years ago. He hadn't changed much since the photo was taken, you know. He had a word or two with Dad — but I don't know if Dad recognized Colin. But I did. I did, as soon as he came in the door.'

'And me?'

'Well, as soon as you spoke and began talking about the picture — well, then I looked at you and reckoned I could place you.' She shook her head slowly, in pleasant recall: 'You and Colin, you know — neither of you — you've not changed so much.'

'Then you're Ed Spencer's daughter — one of his daughters? The blonde one?'

'Daughter-in-law. Old Mr Spencer's dead now. Passed away about a year ago. But Mrs Spencer is still around. She's down shopping in the town. Would you care to drop in and have a word with her, say, after two o'clock?'

I said I would. But I didn't. Dorothy and I walked around some of the streets of Bicester for a while. We saw the old churchyard; and I looked in vain for a house lintel that I had remembered seeing in 1941 as carrying a seventeenth-century date. Then we sat, for my arthritic hips and back were giving me hell. We didn't even get to see the airfield, RAF Bicester, that I had travelled so far to revisit — although the same taxi that had carried us from the railway station to the Fox Inn could as surely have been summoned for the short journey out of town.

A strange melancholy, not altogether born of my physical pain, had descended on me. Maybe it was the finding of that old memento in the tap room of the Fox Inn that made me realize that our distant yesterdays can endure, clear and shining, only in our memories. A return to old haunts cannot conjure back the brave days, for the here-and-the-now intrudes, demandingly busy and impersonal.

Dorothy and I caught an early train back to London. Somehow, my visit to Bicester had ended in an anti-climax. But had it?

It was when I got back to New Zealand that nostalgia again nagged at me, and I was prompted to do something about that crude eulogy I had penned to Ed Spencer. I wrote to the editor of the *Bicester Advertiser* and asked if he would have a photograph taken of the sketch. And if he would be kind enough to send it to me, I would gladly pay the dues.

He did more than that. Within a week or two I received not only a print of the photograph, but a copy of the newspaper which contained a half-page story of how the sketch came to be hanging in the Fox Inn thirty-seven years after it had been designed. And, bless that good editor, there was no fee due.

And perhaps, who knows, the sketch is there today? Maybe those six young New Zealanders in RAF Irvin jackets are still smiling out to meet the gaze of Britons who come to wassail at the Fox Inn?

★ ★ ★

My flying log-book shows me that we six New Zealand sergeant-pilots arrived at No 13 OTU, Bicester, on 16 September 1941, along with twelve Australians, one Canadian, and two lonely Englishmen, who tried to interpret the broad drawls and twangs of colloquialisms tossed back and forthy by their colonial cousins.

On the first day of our arrival on the station, Jack Keys and I wandered along the tarmac and found ourselves inside a hangar, inspecting with some awe a Mark I Blenheim. It was the first operational aircraft we had ever seen at close quarters and the fact that we would soon be expected to fly these monsters made us apprehensive. We stuck our toes in the footholds in the fuselage and climbed, by way of the port wing walkway, into the cockpit. One of us sat on the navigator's jump seat while the other, like a kid with a wondrous toy, pulled and pushed the control column and pumped the throttle levers. Petrol piddled from the disturbed carburetters on to the floor of the hangar.

The Blenheim was a grand aircraft — despite what an academic critic theorized to the contrary when he reviewed one of my recent writings on the machine. It was designed by Frank Barnwell, the Bristol Aeroplane Company's chief designer, and emerged from the prototype of the aircraft ordered by Lord Rothermere — Type 142 — which first flew from Filton in April 1935.

Type 142 aroused such great interest in Air Ministry circles on account of its high performance — its top speed of 307 mph being faster than any contemporary RAF fighter in service — that Lord Rothermere generously presented it to the nation for full evaluation as a potential bomber. And so the Blenheim emerged, and both the Mark I and the Mark IV versions acquitted themselves valiantly. But by the time the Mark V came on the scene, the faithful Blenheim had flown into obsolescence.

I flew solo without any difficulty and was soon ready to collect a crew. During classroom lectures we had been rubbing shoulders with trainee navigators and wireless operator-air gunners and, as the methods of crewing-up were left to personal preferences, pilots would sniff around and sort out likely partners from the selection of navigators. Then, paired off, they would hunt together for a practical and compatible WOP-AG to complete the trio.

My navigator was Les Norman, a nineteen-year-old Londoner who had been a clerk. Ces Dutton was my WOP-AG. He was from Chester and was a prominent cricketer.

Having cut our operational-aircraft teeth on Mark I Blenheims, we continued our training exercises on the long-nose Blenheim IVs — the type we would be flying on 'ops" against enemy defences. We flew several navigation exercises and did much formation flying. We also practised bombing from all heights. But the type of attack that appealed most to me was the low-level run where the pilot released the stick of bombs himself, relying on his own judgement to press the button on the control column at the right moment.

This type of assault, from which the RAF developed its skip-bombing of enemy shipping with eleven-second-delay bombs, was well employed by Blenheim crews off the coast of Holland at the time. The technique required a wave-top run in on the target with much jinking and yawing to dodge — or try to dodge — the usual murderous fire from the ship; and then a straightening for the strike, the release of the bomb load and a smart pull-up to clear the masts and rigging and the inevitable anti-aircraft balloon flying above the vessel.

Avoiding such obstacles, the pilot was then free to push the control column down hard and make for the surface of the sea while the Blenheim's engines, momentarily starved of petrol by the sudden disturbance in the carburettors, would splutter unnervingly for a second or two.

A little later, if the delayed-action bomb had penetrated the hide of the ship, there would be an explosion inside the guts of the vessel, close down by the waterline. But the Blenheim, if it had not been destroyed in the attack, would be clear of the blast and scampering for home amidst a hail of light-cannon fire. The aircraft we flew at Bicester had seen better days. They had, in the main, flown on similar types of missions before being pensioned off to be used by trainee aircrews. And their battle-weary engines, albeit receiving regular inspections and overhauls, were prone to many and mysterious illnesses. The state of fitness of each machine was recorded in its own Form 700, a document usually clamped to a clip-board in the manner of a hospital patient's medical chart — which indeed was what the '700' was in relation to its aircraft.

A pilot, before take-off, would be presented with the 700 by the ground mechanic in charge and invited to sign the document to his satisfaction of the machine's airworthiness. So doing, he thereby technically absolved all others of blame should the aeroplane suffer any airframe or mechanical mishap in flight. But should the pilot discover some malfunction of the machine while in his care, he was also obliged to specify the trouble in writing and sign the 700 to make the aircraft unserviceable — or U/S, in the popular jargon. Thereupon, the ground-staff would have to put matters right before the aeroplane could fly again.

Norman, Dutton and I were detailed to fly our allotted Blenheim G-George on a live-bombing exercise over a missile range somewhere in Wiltshire. On our outward trip I noticed that the port engine's temperature was rising. Not significantly, but sufficient for my more than usual attention to the trembling little finger that pointed to the therm figures on the gauge.

We dropped our live 500-pounder, felt the machine lift appreciably as the burden fell away, and noted with satisfaction the cloud of grey smoke that showed us a close hit on the target. Then I looked again to the port engine's temperature gauge. The needle was now showing a decided climb. We headed for base and arrived with both engines performing well and sounding sweet. But by that time the gauge was giving a very hot reading.

When we climbed out of G-George at dispersal I walked over to the flight hut and asked for the Form 700. I wrote, 'Port engine temperature gauge showing a very high reading,' and, with my signature alongside, made the aircraft U/S.

'How did the engine perform, sergeant?' asked the maintenance NCO in charge of G-George. 'Was it rough? Was it missing at all?'

I told him, no. 'As a matter of fact, it ran well. But it got bloody hot.' And I described the needle's upward climb from time of take-off to our landing.

'Probably the bloody gauge,' he muttered. And he spoke of incapable instrument bashers and the woes that descended upon a flight-sergeant with too much work on his plate. Then he called our little meeting closed and dismissed me with the vague assurance, 'Anyhow, we'll have a look at it.'

The next day we were briefed to fly a navigation exercise and I had drawn A-Apple, a different Blenheim from yesterday's excursion. And as we taxied out towards take-off point, I saw that Blenheim G-George was paused at the end of the grass runway strip as the pilot went through his mnemonic of H-T-M-P-F-F-G — hydraulics, trim, mixture, pitch, fuel, flaps and gills. G-George then began to roll forward, gather speed and become airborne. I watched the control tower, got the green Aldis flash, and it was my turn to move up for take-off and chant my check-list sacrament like a priest before an altar. I called to my two travelling companions over the intercom, 'All set for take-off?'

Yes, they were ready for the aerial road.

So I moved the throttles forward, pointed the aeroplane's snout into the eye of the wind and gunned A-Apple. It moved over the grass as purposefully as any tired Blenheim could, and when we had lift-off I climbed it upwards on the crisp and sunny winter's morning. Up came the wheels and up came the small amount of flap I had used to get an early release from earth. We climbed higher and I reached behind my left hip and groped for the quaint, plunger-type controls that would change my fine pitch to a cruising coarse setting. Then I looked below and saw with horror that G-George, that had taken off just before us, was now flat on its belly in a field and blazing furiously. The first ball of that ugly, black pillar of smoke that attends a petrol fire was rising from the pyre.

My mind did a flip and my stomach was chilled with the realization that it was only yesterday that I had piloted G-George with its hot-reading port temperature gauge. Had the flight-sergeant and his crew really got to the seat of the trouble? Or was he content that it was merely a faulty gauge?

When we landed we found that little Canadian Howie Schraeder and his crew had all perished in the crash. Colin Papps and Dave Wacher, when we discussed the tragedy with them, were very upset. It seems that they had got to the crash site soon after G-George spun in with Howie Schraeder trying to grapple with asymmetric flight after his port engine failed.

'Oh, Jesus. It was terrible!' Colin Papps said. 'The poor buggers were in there, trying to get out, and the bloody fire crew had protective clothing on but they wouldn't go near the fire!'

And it wasn't long after that accident that a Blenheim crashed on the tarmac close to the control tower. The aircraft was carrying a complement of six, all bound on weekend leave for an airfield somewhere south. But the pilot, an instructor at Bicester, had failed to do his cockpit check correctly before take-off. Seemingly, he had wound his stablizer trim-wheel several notches backwards instead of forward. The aircraft had become airborne, but all the strength of Samson could not hold the nose down. The Blenheim rose, stalled and fell back to crash and kill all within it.

Our OTU training at Bicester, in the normal course of events, should have been completed within four or five weeks, but an unusually severe winter with heavy snowfalls had stretched the training period to more than four months. Midway through January 1942 my crewmates and I were sent to the Bristol Aeroplane Company hangars at Filton to collect a reconditioned Blenheim — V-Victor 6257 — which we were to put through petrol consumption tests before proceeding to our posting, a destination in the Middle East by way of Gibraltar and Malta.

I signed a receipt for one reconditioned Blenheim Mk IV aeroplane and one Smith and Wesson calibre .38 pistol — a rather strange coupling of equipment to be drawn from an aeroplane maintenance depot. Presumably the revolver, like the side-arm carried by the now outdated cavalryman, was also a mercy weapon. If my faithful Pegasus should land behind enemy lines and break an oleo leg or fracture a wing through my ill judgement, I could give it the *coup de grâce* before finishing myself with a pistol shot for my sins.

V-Victor 6257 was a good machine. It started well, cruised sweetly without a hiccup and, being easy to trim, it flew true aerodynamically. Adorning its port nose was a large and well-painted picture of Disney's cartoon dog character, Pluto, the creature in a posture of perpetual surprise with its jowls on the ground, its eyes saucer wide, its backside upthrust and its needle tail pointing to the sky. Well might he have shown alarm had he but known the dangers we were to encounter so soon after leaving the Bristol workshops.

We took off from Filton in a bit of a twitter, as the aerodrome was liberally festooned with barrage balloons and we had to steer a very steady and narrow course through their cables. Soon after we set our aircraft down at Bicester we were involved in the petrol tests to ensure we could indeed reach our staging points en route to North Africa. And, as we had so far spent all our flying training on grass airfields, we were required to do a series of circuits and landings on the bitumen runways of Hinton-in-the-Hedges, Bicester's satellite airfield. Hereafter, we were told, all our take-offs and landings would be on hard surfaces — some, of course, being harder than others.

The first leg of our journey, after leaving England, would be the long haul down to Gibraltar and so, in the navigation room at Bicester, we were briefed on the procedures and the perils of not only reaching that rocky outpost but of landing on the airstrip. The flight-sergeant with the half-winged flying 'O' of an observer (custom not having yet blessed him with the later and popular title of navigator) demonstrated, with the help of a large plaster model, whereat lay monsters. A frightful turbulence around the steep lee of the rock could cast us into the sea unless the pilot kept well out of danger by making a final approach akin to a Sunderland skipper reaching for a roadstead touchdown in a fog. Long and low, man, was the recommended drill for survival.

We were very impressed. This was flying of a bold order indeed, spiced with sufficient danger to make it high adventure.

'But it's a piece of cake,' the flight-sergeant assured us. 'Just watch yourself over the Bay of Biscay, though. You'll see a lot of French fishing boats, maybe Spanish, too, and a lot of them are German sympathizers. So the next thing you'll know is a couple of Ju-88s or maybe some Me-110s will be pissing around, in answer to the boats' wireless signals, and you'll be drifting in your life jackets.'

We were not very impressed with this information.

Soon it came the hour for us to leave Bicester. It had been snowing hard for days before our time of departure, so the snow-ploughs had been called in to carve a runway, and high banks of the shovelled stuff were raised each side of the strip, which was now back at grass level, but puddled with large pools of melted slush.

Each aircraft was laden with much-needed spare parts and equipment for Malta and points eastwards. On top of that was each crewman's personal effects, limited by official decree to a certain poundage but, in our case and in ignorance of matters aerodynamic, ridiculously exceeded. An auxiliary petrol tank had also been stuffed into the bomb bay of each transitory aircraft. But, mercifully, it had not been filled for the initial take-off in such appalling conditions.

Sensibly not entrusting the task to raw sergeant-pilots, the senior powers at Bicester called in their more seasoned flying instructors to get the Blenheims airborne from the slushy grass airfield and we stood and watched in awe as the propellers whipped up great sheets of spray and the machines wallowed airborne on their way towards the hard runways at Hinton. We followed in Air Force trucks and, having located our own aeroplanes, took off for Portreath, an airfield on the north-west coast of Cornwall.

We landed with Dutton complaining that his turret hydraulic system was not functioning. And as it was unanimous within our triumvirate that we should not tempt fate or any German fighter by venturing across the Bay of Biscay with our WOP-AG virtually powerless, we called on Portreath's aid. So while Dutton was explaining his worries to the armourers and while the armourers and the maintenance airmen were exploring the big mystery, the station fuel tanker drew up to our Blenheim and began topping up our wing tanks and filling our bomb-bay auxiliary reservoir ready for our early departure the following morning.

The last of the petrol had been pumped aboard V6257 and the Blenheim was resting, fat and heavy with fuel and divers chunks of machinery, on flattening tyres, when the maintenance flight-sergeant sought my attention and said the aircraft would need to be air-tested. Dutton, he explained, could thereby assure himself, his skipper and his navigator that God, with the assistance of 'A' Flight's groundcrew, was back in his heaven, and all within the turret and the hydraulic tubes was working wonderfully.

I said a dirty word and pointed out that the already overloaded machine had just been filled to the tank caps with petrol and would therefore have the gliding angle of a bull turd when I brought it in for a landing.

The flight-sergeant nodded. 'You will have to be very, very careful,' he pointed out, a bit of advice I considered somewhat less than complimentary to my judgement. 'But the only way your WOP-AG can satisfy himself about his turret working in action is by way of an air test.'

The nub of all his concern lay in the fact that the Blenheim's hydraulic system was shared by both the pilot and the turret gunner — but not at the same time. The pilot needed the juices to raise his undercarriage and flaps after the machine became airborne. And when he had got everything tucked snugly inboard, he moved a plunger and let his gunner have uninterrupted control of the hydraulic power until it was time to go into the landing pattern again, and the lowering of the wheels and flaps.

Dutton and I climbed into the aeroplane. We left Norman, smiling smugly, on the tarmac. Even his spindly 135-pound frame was just too much extra weight to take aboard.

The runway in use led to a sudden drop at the windward end — a feature I had noticed as I had made my exploratory survey of the airfield before landing from our run from Hinton. And now I viewed this as a fortuitous piece of luck. The Blenheim waddled like a fat duck towards the take-off end and, with great deliberation I recited my cockpit drill. I engaged the plus-nine manifold pressure tit which would give me emergency power and the aircraft rumbled along into wind, gained flying speed and left the runway just before we ran out of tarseal.

I gasped with surprise as the land suddenly fell away below us and we were aloft over the edge of the cliff, the Blenheim wallowing and sinking for an awful moment before it gained airspeed and reached for altitude.

Dutton's turret worked well and we came in for our landing. But my fears of the maching falling out of my hands were ill-founded. I motored V6257 down to the deck with plenty of airspeed and pulled off a rather good touchdown.

Blenheim Mk. I.

6
Outward Bound

On the morning of 29 January 1942, with an early breakfast of scrambled powdered-egg on toast still churning within our excited stomachs, and our in-flight rations tucked under our arms, we clumped our way to V6257's dispersal point. Norman and Dutton wore their parachute harness and carried their detachable packs while I shouldered my pilot-type 'chute. My throne in the Blenheim was what we called a bucket seat. Into this basin would go the pack of my parachute, and on this knobbly cushion I would have to sit for the duration of my flight. In this case, it was going to be a long flight — about eight hours, by Les Norman's calculations.

And as the pack also contained an ill-folded inflatable rubber dinghy, my backside, I knew, was going to be very tender by the time we got to Gibraltar. I had had my assurances of that *en route* from Hinton, a mere hop of only two hours.

V6257's two radial Mercury-15 motors started without demur and, buoyant of spirit and vulgar with braggadocio, we exchanged witticisms as the cylinders warmed and it was time to run up each engine to plus-five boost and test for magneto drop.

Everything was fine. I waved away the chocks and we were off on our high adventure. Now boldly confident of the Blenheim's ability to become airborne with its extra fuel, I gave it the gun with full plus-nine power, and old V6257 left England and wallowed as the ground gave way to open space above the cliff. It rose triumphantly, obeyed my commands on the controls and, as I pointed its nose towards Land's End, its crew sighed relief in unison, and again made repartee over the intercom.

Both engines were purring sweetly as we left the last rock of England behind and faced the open sea of Biscay. Somewhat subdued by the tales we had been told of the Luftwaffe's bandits, we searched the wide and clear blue sky, and chided God for not donating even a wisp of cloud cover.

'Is your turret still working?' I asked Dutton. He had earlier tested his guns. But I was nervous of another hydraulic failure.

'Aye.' Dutton was an inland Chester man, but he invariably responded to inquiry like a true mariner.

'Better keep it what way,' I said. 'We're now in the danger zone. And those ambitious Jerry pilots like to mix it with sprog transit crews. So watch the skies.'

'That's what I'm here for,' Dutton muttered.

Les Norman was sitting on the jump-seat beside me. He had done his navigation sums for the while and was taking the sunshine before it came time for him to work the wobble-pump and transfer petrol from the bomb-bay reservoir to the emptying wing tanks.

He was the first to see the glint of sun on the aircraft's cockpit canopy. He yelled: 'Bogey, bogey!' He punched my right arm and pointed towards the hazy distance wherein lay the coast of France — and from out of which a menacing Junkers-88 was advancing towards us at speed.

I wrenched the Blenheim to starboard in a wicked turn, pointed it in the general direction of America and dived for the surface of the sea, a first-priority drill that had been instilled in us as removing one of the enemy's dimensions. He could not get under us to hit our unprotected belly. Also, he dare not continue a downward dive on us for long, otherwise he might not be able to pull out in time before he hit the water.

Now flying at twenty or thirty feet above the waves, I sought some information from my gunner. 'Where's he now, Dut?' I barked. 'Keep me . . .'

A seam of white lace was sewn to the blue surface of the sea. It began just forward of my left wing and then frothed away to port at an angle. There was no need to ask. The bastard had made a diving pass at my starboard quarter. Then the ugly shape of the German aircraft swept overhead, following the welts of foam left by his forward guns. And the Angel of Death went climbing upwards.

I kept on flying us seawards and away from danger as fast as the

Blenheim could trundle. And then Dutton called that the enemy had decided to return to the Continent. Like us, his would-be prey, he had to consider his fuel reserves. So I pulled back the power that was grinding the engines towards sudden debility and lifted the Blenheim to the more comfortable height of one thousand feet, and an airspeed more compatible with the aircraft's age and burden. Les Norman then returned to his tiny compartment in the aircraft's nose and got involved with his chart and his navigational problems. And soon he produced a new course for me to steer.

Then, with the danger past, badinage bubbled from our lips in over-loquacity, as urgent as the tributaries of a stream too long dammed will rush, on release, to find a level. And we found it. We were again a trio of rather coarse little men, rejoicing in our doubtful skills and our everlasting good fortune with the vulgarity of urchins. Out from the recesses of recall came the bawdy ditties we had heard and memorized in Bicester taverns and the airmen's and sergeants' messes of the stations we had inhabited. And we, a discordant trio in the middle of the Bay of Biscay and entertaining none but ourselves, sang of Salome, the good ship Venus and the ship that was leaving Bombay.

I called Les Norman and he again took his seat beside me and began his task of pumping fuel from the bomb-bay to the emptying wing tanks. Still in brilliant sunshine we continued southwards down the coast of Portugal and I groaned from buttock to buttock as the knobs and folds of the tight-packed rubber dinghy impressed intaglio replicas on my backside. We beamed Cape St Vincent on our port and we rumbled onwards into the Gulf of Cadiz. Six hours had gone slowly by — seven hours. We came up to the Spanish headland of Tarifa at the portals of the Strait of Gibraltar and then, dimly on the port bow, we beheld the out-thrust of Europa Point and, behind it, the outline of the fabulous Rock of Gibraltar.

It was a travel-book picture made actual and the three of us burst into chatter. The first long leg of our eastward journey was all but completed and here we were, intact and in person, at the fabled gateway to the Mediterranean.

We were challenged by the diligent watchkeepers at the Point and we returned to them, by way of a Very pistol flare, our identification colours of the day. And we prayed that their aircraft-recognition vigilantes could tell a Blenheim from a Messerschmitt or a Junkers.

I brought our V6257 around to port and approached the awesome

Rock at about one thousand feet. The sea's surface had indicated the wind direction, and as there was but one runway at Gibraltar, I had the choice of only two directions for landing. Taking the one nearer to the wind's eye, I would approach from the Mediterranean end and therefore the lee of the precipitous east face of the Rock would be harbouring the dreaded turbulence that the flight-sergeant had spoken of.

Even Dutton, probably as much removed from matters aerodynamic as any turret-bound WOP-AG, had much counsel to offer me as we drew near the gigantic upthrust. 'Mind the turbulence, skipper,' and 'Don't get too close to the east face, skipper,' were ready and oft-repeated instructions as I moved the Blenheim into position for my landing pattern.

From a position well out to sea I let down the undercarriage and sufficient flap to have the aircraft under steady control as we descended in our long and low final approach. I watched, with eyes that flicked upwards and downwards like a pair of signalling Aldis lamps, the end of the runway and the airspeed indicator needle. My left hand on the throttles was giving and taking power, and the brave engines were responding. My right hand was juggling the control column, picking up a dipping wing and balancing the machine fore and aft to keep us on a steady and safe descent.

I let down full flap and soon the breakwater rocks whipped below us and we were above the runway. I cut back power and, with both hands on the control column grips, I jockeyed to meet the asphalt. The Blenheim, as though thoroughly exhausted, fell willingly to earth, bounced once and ran its distance.

The flight from Portreath had taken us eight hours and ten minutes, the longest flight I had, at that stage, undertaken. But the sum total of my flying time to that date was a modest 207 hours. I had had my first brush with the enemy before I had flown 200 hours, and already my crew and I felt like seasoned combatants.

But, so early in our flying careers, we were very naïve.

We found two fellow crews from Bicester at Gibraltar awaiting repairs to their Blenheims before they should again be on their separate ways eastwards. Sergeant-pilots Stokes and 'Gooney' Jeffries, both Australians, had successfully skippered their aircraft to the Rock, but were now languishing in the winter sun while the groundcrews laboured over the sick Mercury-15 engines. Having been at the airstrip for the past two days, they showed us the delights of the

British outpost with the sophisticated airs of long-experienced travellers. We wandered through the narrow shopping lanes and climbed upwards along zig-zagging paths to vantage spots from where we could see far over the Bay de Algeciras and the broad landscape of Spain. Away to the south, across the Strait of Gibraltar, lay Morocco.

We were indeed in strange latitudes. For us, war with its adventures and fortunes and fears had just begun.

We were at Gibraltar for two nights and one full day, a period we felt as quite sufficient for our recuperation. It would not have mattered one whit had we felt otherwise, for on the morning of 3 January we were summoned to a briefing at the OC's office and told that three of our serviceable Blenheims were to fly together to Malta, the second stop on our scheduled transit flight to the Middle East.

Blenheim Mk. IV approaching Gibraltar.

At Malta, so the story went, we would be provided with maps and we would be given specific instructions as to our final destination in North Africa, and the means by which we could recognize the place.

'Now,' said the senior RAF officer, 'off you go.'

Off we went. A flight-lieutenant, whose name escapes me, for the introduction was cool and brief, was to lead us, and Stokes and I would follow obediently as, respectively, his numbers two and three.

We took off singly at an early hour, the proposed drill being a rendezvous over the peak of the Rock, when we would get ourselves into loose formation and proceed to Malta. But when Stokes and I arrived at the trysting place, there was no sign of the flight-lieutenant's aircraft.

We circled fruitlessly for a few minutes. Then Stokes' voice came drawling over the RT. 'Ji-um! We're using up too much juice, buggering around like this. How's about us pissing off by ourselves?'

I agreed. So Stokes set off eastwards and I tucked our aircraft close to his starboard quarter. We were to learn later that the flight-lieutenant's Blenheim had developed engine trouble on take-off and he had had to make a smart emergency landing. And a stern rebuke for our setting off into danger as an ill-prepared pair was awaiting us when we landed, a signal having preceded us to Malta.

The sky over the Mediterranean was clear and the sea mirrored it as a dream scene in azure. Our two Blenheims, rising and sinking to the whims of thermal airs, were the only intruders in this blue paradise. Off to our right, seen dimly, was the Algerian coastline with the headland of Mers el Kebir coming up to align with our starboard wingtip.

Of a sudden Dutton's voice came loud and urgent through the intercom. 'Two aircraft approaching fast at four o'clock high. Range half a mile!' And his message was almost clipped short by Stokes calling on RT: 'Fighters coming at us on the starboard quarter. Let's get cracking fast!' He turned port through forty-five degrees and bore away from the hostile land. And when he said 'fast' he surely meant it, for he had obviously slammed in his plus-nine boost. I followed procedure and followed Stokes, tucking my port wingtip so close to his fuselage that I almost scored a bullseye on the roundel.

Ces Dutton and Stokes' WOP-AG kept feeding us their commentaries. But gradually the urgency left their voices and when they reported that the attackers — presumably Vichy French — had left us, we took off emergency power and relaxed a little.

Nothing further annoyed or alarmed us until we drew close to the enemy island of Pantelleria. An Italian float-plane of the Cant breed crossed our bows at a distance of about two thousand yards. It is debatable whether the two Blenheim crews or the men aboard the Cant were the more concerned. At all events it must have been mutually decided to let sleeping dogs lie, each side no doubt being somewhat unsure of the calibre and firepower of the other. I know, for

At 13 OTU, Bicester, in 1941: The author (left) and fellow New Zealander, Jack Keys.

Glenn Martin Baltimores flying over the pyramids, circa 1942.

A Glenn Martin Maryland of 203 Squadron, Burg el Arab, with aircrew and groundcrew members. Sergeants Dutton and Norman are second and third from left.

Toby Webster, the author's great mate, who was killed at Gibraltar, January 1943.

Sergeant-pilot Snibbo Baum at Burg el Arab.

Dorothy, the London girl I married in 1943.

my part, I was more than happy to let the enemy go crusing by
unmolested and unmolesting.

Our two aircraft came up on the coast of Malta with our IFF
(Identification, Friend or Foe) transmitters bleeping out our most
friendly intentions and, in obedience of our briefings at Gibraltar, we
began circling and shooting off our Very cartridge colours-of-the-day.
We got an acknowledgement and an invitation to land. And we were
heading thankfully towards the island and the Luqa airfield when an
Aldis lamp on the shore began flickering a message. My twelve-
words-a-minute knowledge of Morse was put to its first wartime test.

'What's he say, what's he say?' Norman and Dutton chorused.

I interpreted the message to them, letter by letter: 'H-U-R-R-Y.'

We arrived at Luqa in air astir with ack-ack missiles from the
island's defence posts, and landed urgently on a runway already blue-
misted with gunsmoke. A lone groundcrew sergeant in dirty khaki
battledress and wearing a tin helmet was showing agitation as he
beckoned us to a temporary dispersal point. Then, by signals, he
invited us to follow him with all haste. I cut power from the engines
and the three of us left the Blenheim at speed as bombs began to fall
on the airfield.

So this was what the Aldis-lamp signaller meant when he urged
'Hurry'. In the air-raid shelter we learned that the airfield was
experiencing its third bombing that day. 'You jes' made it in time,
sarge,' a Malta-seasoned corporal told me. 'Uvverwise you might'a
been anuvver bloomin' roundel painted on the scoreboard of some
Jerry's kite.'

We met up with Stokes and his crew, who had arrived immediately
ahead of us and, after we had reported our arrival and received our
scoldings, we were dispatched to our billets — a ward in what had
been the island's poorhouse hospital before the RAF had acquired it
as a dormitory for its 'other ranks.' It was there, too, that we met
Snibbo Baum and his two crewmates.

Right from the time of our agitated arrival at Luqa, I took a decided
dislike to Malta, an opinion certainly not mellowed by our introduction
to the sleeping quarters allotted us. Gloom, like a dirty grey blanket,
seemed to hang over everything in the building, from the vacant
stretcher-beds of recently deceased aircrews to the sad, pallid
sandstone walls that proclaimed the place a prison of the soul.

However, we rallied our tired bodies and spirits sufficiently to
travel into Valletta for the evening and, inevitably, to wander down

into the seamy, narrow Strada Stredda which was long known to Royal Navy men as 'The Gut'. And, just as inevitably, we moved from one disgusting pub to another, drinking strange wartime concoctions and imagining, for an hour or two, that we were having the time of our young lives.

And, seeing the limits of Malta's offerings in rest and recreation, we rejoiced in knowing that the terms of our transit flight decreed that we would soon be on our way to the Middle East.

Blenheim Mk. IV.

7

General Reconnaissance

Established within 203 Squadron at Burg el Arab after our dramatically-ended flight from Malta, and our concentrated course in flying the Maryland, my crew and I found ourselves still very much in the role of trainee aircrew. Baum and his lads had also been posted to 203 Squadron and the six of us found ourselves immersed in an on-squadron course that was to shape us into general reconnaissance airmen. As our future flying work would see us closely associated with the Royal Navy, we were required to attend classes in dead-reckoning navigation, patrol and search procedures, ship recognition, reconnaissance, Navy coding, meteorology and Navy signals. We all passed with reasonable marks and we all cribbed shamelessly, pre-penning our key answers on the white skin of our thighs just hidden by the leg-lines of our shorts.

We were allotted tents on the edge of a rocky *wadi* — which, in Egyptian, meant any depression from a slight hollow to a ravine — and we soon found that the ugly scorpions that abound in the stony wilderness showed a fondness for the warmth of our beds and our boots. So the old domestic ritual of putting the cat out each night became a careful shaking of our blankets before we bedded down. And each morning our boots were vigorously pounded to dislodge any invaders.

Les Norman and Ces Dutton and I shared out tent with a flight-sergeant named Heyward, a bit of a recluse and a pilot without a crew. We had acquired him along with the tent to which we had been directed when we arrived at the airfield. Heyward was a reasonably long-serving member of the squadron and, from what we could gather, his crew had flown with another captain one day and had not returned from the patrol. So now Heyward was learning to fly one of the few Marylands so far allocated to the unit, in readiness for the time he might take over another crew.

While he was practising his Maryland circuits-and-bumps one afternoon, Norman and I were in our tent studying our ship-recognition assignments. The circuit pattern had the aircraft taking off almost over our heads and we would casually observe, as the engines roared with power and fine-pitched propellers above us: 'There goes old Heyward again.'

Later in the exercise, when the pilot was practising overshoots, we heard the muted sounds of the aircraft coming in on the final approach, followed by the burst of power as Heyward gave it the gun to go around again. The Maryland came over our tent, roaring like a banshee. And then came the ominous, sudden silence that could only mean a stall.

We scrambled to the tent flap in time to see the aeroplane hit the ground and immediately burst into a gigantic ball of fire. *Whoomph!* It was the most ghastly sight I have ever seen. And it happened right before our eyes only two hundred metres from our tent.

We raced down the shallow *wadi* where Heyward's funeral pyre roared, sending upwards its hideous, dense pillar of black smoke. Every man on the station was following us. We got as close to the wreck as we could, but the heat was terrible. The squadron's fire tender came clattering over the boulders and camel thorn, and its crew tried to get some foam onto the inferno. But the fire was furious, far and away beyond stay as it fed on the high-octane aviation fuel.

And in the middle of the furnace we could see the hunched remains of Flight-sergeant Heyward.

A petrol tank that had not exploded with the impact of the crash now sent a massive gout of flame and its contribution of black smoke high into the desert air. The aircraft's supply of Very cartridges added a macabre pyrotechnical display to this Viking's funeral. And, as the fire roasted it to unbearable limits, the oxygen supply tank exploded like a bomb, scattering some of the helpless watchers in alarm.

Dutton, who had been engrossed in a lecture on wireless procedures when the crash happened, now joined us as we wandered, shaken and white-faced, back to our tent. 'This war's getting bloody dangerous,' he murmured. We didn't say anything. We just nodded.

I had been on the squadron for about three weeks before I met the commanding officer, Wing Commander Johnson. I came upon him one morning as he was relieving himself at one of the gonophones which were conveniently placed around the camp. These urinals, in the form of open-ended pedestals, were assembled from two or three four-gallon petrol cans, the outlet end being placed over a sump-hole in the porous sand. Crude and public though they may have been, they encouraged the troops away from peeing haphazardly around tent sites, there being a decided absence of shrubbery at Burg el Arab.

I saluted as I walked by. But as the CO's right hand was otherwise engaged, he refrained from returning the compliment, choosing to gaze towards the heat-hazed horizon. I was about to proceed onwards when he called to me: 'Sanders, isn't it?'

I told him, yessir, it was. He buttoned his fly and beckoned me closer. 'Sanders,' he said. 'I see you have been going over my head and writing to your RNZAF Headquarters in London about some promotion you feel is your due. Correct?'

'Yes, sir,' I answered, I had done that. I explained that I had met one of my fellow New Zealand contemporaries while on leave in Cairo. He had been promoted to flight-sergeant a month earlier and was surprised that I was still a sergeant. He had told me that all I had to do was write to RNZAF Headquarters in London, whereupon I would be granted my 'crowns' as I was a New Zealander and subject to RNZAF terms of enlistment.

'Well, Sanders, I shall personally see that your promotion is withheld for six months as a punishment for your impudence,' he said.

I had been stupidly naïve on two counts. Protocol and military law say that a serviceman shall not apply for anything but through his commanding officer. Secondly, none but an idiot would put such a request as mine in letter form if he but realized that all wartime mail in and out of a unit is censored.

Wing Commander Johnson was true to his word. Time was to show that I was still a sergeant months after my associates were getting the few extra bob of a flight-sergeant every pay day.

We continued to fly Blenheims for a few weeks after we joined 203 Squadron. We searched along our anti-submarine 'crabs', flew our convoy patrols and our daylight reconnaissance sorties over the Mediterranean. One memorable night we took off in one of several Blenheims to try and skip-bomb an enemy tanker that was expected to leave Greece with petrol for Rommel's Afrika Corps. But we found nothing and, at the limits of our fuel endurance, we returned for a dawn touch-down. One of our party had an airscrew fly off in mid-air, but the weary Blenheim managed to make land before belly-flopping. Our machines, tired by time and cylinder-scoured by desert sand, did not give satisfactory one-engine performances.

Although our primary role was that of daylight reconnaissance — certainly more defensive than offensive — we were, on occasions, given depth charges when our briefing called for a search for submarines. Early in June 1942, Norman, Dutton and I were on such a quest. Reports had advised sightings of a U-boat and we were given an area to patrol. Towards the end of our search Dutton sighted a small flurry on the surface. We turned and ran up on the spot. There was an oil slick which suggested the submarine might be damaged, possibly from an earlier attack by some other aircraft. We straddled the spot with our depth charges, saw the violent eruptions of white water, and circled the area for as long as our diminishing fuel would permit, looking for evidence of a hit. Certainly, the oil slick seemed to be spreading wider. But we could no longer linger and, unfortunately, could not claim a successful strike.

About a month after this we were flying Marylands on the long-range reconnaissance flights that took us out to Crete in our searchings for German convoys. From Burg el Arab we would fly to our forward operating base at Sidi Barrani and, on detachment there for about a week or ten days, we would follow up the signalled advice that the Malta-based Photographic Reconnaissance Unit planes had sent of their findings.

Life at Sidi Barrani — up in 'the blue' — was rather more primitive than our days spent at Burg el Arab. Our communal mess, with no deference to rank, was a dugout with sand-bagged entrance through which commissioned officers and NCOs came and went in the somewhat wild dishabille they chose when away from the more formal conditions of base.

Baum was most impressed with the sand bags. 'Remember the movies we saw of soldiers in sand-bagged dugouts?' he marvelled. 'Gawd, I never would'a believed I'd be sitting in a dugout like that myself!'

For my part, I didn't find it all that glamorous. We drank tea made from brackish water, ate bully beef made from genuine rutted-out old bulls and munched on stone-hard biscuits that came in large tins labelled (to my annoyance and embarrassment) as being made in

New Zealand. Such vegetable fodder that we were served came in the form of dehydrated potato chunks captured, as our RAF cook informed us, from a German ration depot.

Between times, after a few trips up in the blue, we would get a brief period of leave in either Cairo or Alexandria where we would feed hungrily on egg-dominated meals pungent with oriental cooking oils. And we would drink much of the local Stella beer, lively with effervescence but lacking in alcohol. Also, we bought plenty of books and magazines to stockpile as avidly as any squirrels hoarding acorns. And because of my artistic aspirations, I invested in pencils, crayons, drawing paper and even some oil paints and canvas-boards.

Baum, who was married to an extraordinarily pretty London girl named Kathleen, persuaded me to copy, in colour, a small black-and-white photo of her. I obliged him (or tried to) by sketching a crayon portrait of the girl. But as I attempted the work at night in flickering, dim yellow light — one candlepower, to be precise — the morning sunshine showed his Kath with such a saffron complexion as would make a Chinese crone positively dough-faced by comparison.

Baum was polite in his acceptance and vowed he would send the picture to his loved one. But if he did, I certainly did not get any fan mail from London. Nor did my attempts at oil painting reach any artistic heights, and I was soon to discover that the Western Desert was hardly conducive to dabbling in that medium. My first picture of a Cairo street scene received a heavy veneer of wind-blown desert sand soon after the first coat of slow-drying pigment was laid. Thereafter, my tubes of colour lay neglected like a nest of crushed, multi-hued slugs.

Baum and I had made mutual promises that, should one of us fail to return from a flight or by any other means reach that great Hereafter, the other would immediately write to the next of kin, and try to compose some explanatory and comforting words on paper. I was then single and so I gave Baum my mother's address. He wanted me to write to his Kath — by which time, presumably, she would have forgotten or forgiven my artistic assaults.

I was to be taxed with that sorrowful task before many weeks had passed.

But, as events was to prove, it could easily have been Baum's lot to write a note to New Zealand. With Rommel pushing eastwards in June 1942, we were hurriedly encouraged by Luftwaffe bombers to move our headquarters from Burg el Arab to an airfield known as LG-X, close to Ismailia on the banks of the Suez Canal.

That meant that every aircraft that could get airborne, including those still under repair, had to be flown to our new home. So there were some hair-raising take-offs as aged Blenheims and sick Marylands managed to stagger into the air and clatter their way across the date palms and paddy fields.

Having done my share of nursing two spluttering, back-firing old Blenheims from Burg el Arab to LG-X, I settled in with my crew in our new surroundings, while we awaited our turn to continue flying our patrols.

From LG-X we would move on operational detachment as far westward as Rommel would permit and, for a period of about ten days or a fortnight, we would press on with our reconnaissance flights over the Mediterranean.

I had, by this time, acquired a small mongrel pup of the terrier type. We named him Pete, gave him Yankee canned beer, which he drank greedily and shamelessly from a saucer and, as he so considered himself so manly, we took him on a few coast-wise flights, chaperoned within the air-gunner's compartment of the Maryland by Dutton and Mike Conway, our new fourth man in the crew.

On our next scheduled operational flight we loaded our gear and ammunition, along with a bag of mail for the aircrews and ground-crews on detachment, into Maryland P-Peter and set off on our westland flight. Pete, as usual, was in the dorsal turret area along with Ces Dutton and Conway.

I went through my cockpit check at the end of the airstrip and rolled the Maryland forward into wind. Advancing the port throttle slightly ahead of the starboard knob to counter the inherent tendency of the aircraft to bear to the left, I gave power and we picked up speed. But something was wrong, and I was fighting to keep the machine straight. It kept bearing to port, although by this time I had given the left engine almost full throttle. The tail came up, but it was now certain that rudder control could not keep the Maryland on a straight course. I ripped the throttles closed. But the aircraft was now committed to the swing and, at much speed, it ground-looped, tearing off its undercarriage and sprawling spectacularly on its belly.

Inevitably, it burst into fire as ruptured fuel lines hosed petrol onto the confused electrical wiring. The four of us leaped for the safety hatches and got clear as the flames woofed around the seats of our pants.

Ces Dutton had had the foresight to lift Pete the pup through the open dorsal turret. The dog had been tied by a piece of rope to the Browning gun mountings, and he hung and struggled by the neck until I ran back through the heat and smoke to cut him free.

The Maryland burned itself into not much more than a couple of blackened motors and a tangle of ribs and longerons. It took with it all our gear and, of course, the bag of mail which we had on board for the men at the forward area.

The station fire engine was, unfortunately, undergoing repairs at the time of the crash, and the frustrated crew had to stand helplessly and watch the petrol tanks blow up without having so much as a bucket of water to toss into the inferno.

After the bits and pieces of the Maryland that had been scattered and unburned had been collected and examined, it was found that the left wheel's brake had partially seized, thereby accounting for my inability to hold the aircraft straight on take-off. We always had a lot of trouble with sand getting into the moving parts of aircraft — the engines of the Blenheims being particularly vulnerable, so that large Vokes filters were standard desert equipment on the air-intake vents of those aircraft.

It was not long before I was in the air again. After a week's leave in Tel Aviv and a visit to Jerusalem, I returned to the squadron, got a Maryland into the sky alone without breaking anything, and was considered capable of venturing with my crew again over the Mediterranean Sea.

Although we of lesser ranks did not know of General Montgomery's plans to stand firm at El Alamein — so near to our old stamping ground of Burg el Arab — we did at least have an inkling that something big was cooking in the military pot. We were again moved westward, fractionally, it is true, to an airfield called Gianaclis on the western edge of the Delta, and the squadron was busily engaged in reconnaissance flights that took us to the islands off the southern coast of Crete.

We saw Vailland crash in flames. And there were other fatalities we did not witness. Towards the end of October 1942 Les Norman was asked to fly as a replacement for another navigator who was ill. It was Les's first — and last — operational flight without me as his pilot. The Maryland he was navigating was briefed to fly a reconnaissance sortie to within a mile or two of the island of Gavdhos, near Crete. It did not return. Our intelligence officer said that the aircraft's IFF signals ceased abruptly when the Maryland would have been somewhere near the outermost extremity of its patrol. The supposition was that it had either been bounced by enemy aircraft, or had hit the water while flying at wave-top height.

The low-flying tactics that we adopted to get below the enemy's radar screen could, and often did, prove hazardous. With a smooth sea below him, a pilot often had difficulty in gauging just how low he was flying and photographs, taken from our own aircraft above, had shown the propeller-wash leaving a distinct wake of ripples behind such a surface-hugger.

I felt unutterably sad and sick after the loss of Les. His nineteen-year-old life would have been snuffed immediately when the Perspex nose compartment of the Maryland hit the water. He would have had no way of escape.

8

A Mediterranean Cruise

They who go down to the sea in ships and occupy their business in great waters may see the works of the Lord and his wonders in the deep. They take their lot of wind and water, playing deadly games of fetch-and-carry and hide-and-seek, while the push and pull of desert warfare has the armies of both sides chafing their ways through sand. The Mediterranean Sea, long alive with action since the sailings of the ancient Greeks and the Phoenicians, is now filled with the wonders of modernity, if not the works of the Lord.

Field-Marshal Rommel's supplies for his desert army come by sea; as indeed do those of the British. The Axis supply routes through the Mediterranean before December 1941 began at Naples and made their way past Sicily, either to westward or through the Strait of Messina, to the North African port of Tripoli. Depending on the fortunes of the see-saw battles, the port of Benghazi could also be a destination.

After 1941, however, the enemy's supply lanes, beginning at either Taranto or Brindisi at the south-east end of Italy, have hugged the western coast of Axis-occupied Greece and swung wide of Malta to bear towards Benghazi and come, due west, to Tripoli.

But what does a humble seaman see of a war?

If he holds the fervour of religion strong in his heart he knows, unquestionably, that God is on his side and that the evils of Satan possess the enemy. If he is an Italian youth, impressed to serve in one of Rommel's tankers, he looks up at the many-splendoured night of moon and a myriad stars and he listens, during his watch on deck, for the dreaded voom-voom-voom of a Bristol Beaufort torpedo-bomber's engines. And he crosses himself and prays to his Almighty to keep him safe from the harm of the merciless British.

If the watcher of the night is a Briton manning a Bofers gun on the deck of a Malta-bound merchantman, he calls on his Lord — who is, of course, an Englishman — to pilot him towards a safe harbour.

Both of these men go to church when they are home from sea. They put their modest offerings into a plate or a box each Sunday. And their mothers and fathers — and their wives and children, too, if they are so blessed — part with small and very precious coins to help the many causes that are the cares of Christendom. And while these men are at sea they try in every way to shape up to the severe requirements of their faiths. They do not swear as much as the coarser of their shipmates, and they try so hard to abstain from the carnal temptations that await far-wandering men in strange and sinful ports. They write home, laboriously and punctiliously, and they keep on saying their prayers.

Each has been assured that the Lord is his shepherd and that, therefore, he shall not want. Each, because he has paid and prayed for it, has a legitimate lien on God's mercy. Between them, and their respective claims and counter-claims, they cause much confusion in Heaven.

Their ships carry them onward through the ever-haunted night; and another age of darkness has been conquered. But what of the dawn?

Around the convoy cargo vessels of both combatant forces weave their guardian destroyer escorts; and below the waves, nosing for openings so that they can run their torpedoes into the ships' guts, ferret the hostile submarines. Above them, looking for tell-tale periscopes or sky attackers, shuttle watchdog aircraft. And a mile or so away, up-sun of these modern argosies and their attendants, lurks the prying, gossip-whispering enemy reconnaissance aeroplane, its bomb bay filled with auxiliary petrol tanks to allow it to linger longer and wireless its findings back to base.

We have been briefed to fly Maryland AH364 in search of an enemy convoy that our intelligence section says should be south of Sapientza, at the bottom tip of Greece, by about 1100 hours. This information has been sent to us by coded signal and the fountainhead, as usual, is one of the Photographic Reconnaissance Unit Spitfires based at Malta. The admirable Wing Commander Adrian Warburton has been keeping a vigilant eye and carefully focused camera lens on this enemy excursion, from the dockside loadings at Brindisi and Taranto to the flotilla's crawl down past Corfu and Cephalonia.

The ships, he reports, were off the Grecian island of Zante and heading southwards at such-and-such a time. At their estimated trudge of about eleven knots they should be clear of the Axis-held coast of Greece and standing to open sea in such-and-such a position by an estimated hour. A daylight reconnaissance check on the convoy's composition, disposition, course and speed is required, so that the torpedo-bombers can go in for the kill at night, with flares and Leigh lights illuminating the targets.

We are to fly by dead reckoning navigation to the estimated area wherein the ships should lie, beginning our diverging or parallel-track or closed-Y search until we find the enemy. And then we are to sneak in as close as possible at wave-top height, assess the size, course and speed of the flotilla, withdraw temporarily, climb to a practical height for wireless transmission and send home our Navy-coded first-sighting report. Then, unless we are sent scurrying by the escort fighters or shot down, we are to continue shadowing the merchant-men and their guardians, transmitting our amplifying signals that could possibly correct or augment our first-sighting information.

On such trips we are usually in the air for about seven hours. We must watch our fuel levels and not outstay our flight endurance. Sergeant Hall, my temporary navigator since Les Norman's ill-starred flight, has been briefed and with dead-reckoning efficiency has laid off his courses with pencil and parallel rule, and has pricked and spanned his chart with dividers, measuring the nautical miles. Ces Dutton and Mike Conway have checked their turret Brownings and their ammunition. They have got their wirless signal codes buttoned up; and their hand-held camera is loaded with film.

We stack ourselves and our gear into the Maryland. Each parachute pack has its own inflatable life raft attached. The day is warm, but we wear our khaki woollen battle-dress uniforms. For if we ditch and are fortunate enough to survive the impact, the nights will be cold as we drift sodden on the sea. Our life jackets, borrowing their sobriquet from that notable and well-endowed film star of the late 1930s, Mae West, are harnessed around our chests like yellow brassieres that hammock gargantuan bosoms.

It is unmercifully hot, for already the sun has climbed in the morning sky and is throwing its rays onto the aircraft. Hall has climbed up the small drop-ladder and has entered his navigation chamber in the nose section through the bottom hatch. He has pulled up the trap after him and is busying himself at his small table. Dutton and Conway, also, have entered their self-contained compartment aft of my cockpit and they, like Hall, have clambered in through a nether trapdoor. We put on our soft leather helmets, plug in our intercom connections and test clarity and strength of our vocal messages. 'Testing, testing. One — two — three — four. . . ' The top line is 'five by five' and we all 'read' it.

The groundcrew boys are below and they have just finished their pre-flight ministrations. Soon they will give us their thumbs-up signal. Soon? We hope so, for the sun of tropical Egypt belts down on our bundled, sweating bodies and the Maryland expands under the heat with a million little tick-tick-tick protests. It is far too hot to linger here.

We get the all-clear signal and I give the port engine power. The airscrew turns over slowly at first, gathering revolutions. Then combustion is caught and there is a bellow of blue-smoked energy as the cylinders spew out their dross. And soon the starboard motor is firing and the oil is circulating and the cylinder-head temperatures are climbing up the gauges. I pull back the control column tight against my belly to anchor the elevators and I run up each engine to take-off boost, testing the switches for magneto drop. The angry air of the slipstream buffets the rudder and elevator surfaces and I feel the protests on the foot pedals and the stick.

Each engine shows a satisfactory accounting of itself, I wave away the wheel chocks and we move out towards the take-off end of the airstrip. We tarry as I check my cockpit drill and search the sky for any incoming traffic. The way is clear and I ease the Maryland around into wind and let it run forward a yard or two to get the tail wheel straight.

'Okay?' I call to my crew. 'All set for take-off?'

Yes, they are ready.

I ease the throttles forward, advancing port power a bit to offset any swing to the left — a favoured trick of the Maryland — and we roll, faster and faster. The aircraft's tail comes up and I have rudder control of the machine. We are making a tremendous amount of dust, I know. But that is whirling and billowing behind us and I am concentrating on what lies ahead, flicking my eyes down to check my instruments, holding the aeroplane straight by rudder control, feeling for the moment when this bellowing metal machine will want to break free of the ground and marry itself to air.

We lift and rise. Now clear of the dusty, dun desert, I reach down and take up the undercarriage and pull back some of the power from the engines. We continue to climb and I twist the grid ring of my compass and clamp it, obeying the course instructions that Sergeant Hall has given me. For double reference I adjust my gyro direction-finder to coincide with the compass heading.

We come to the coast. Below us, the Mediterranean Sea is a fabulous shade of turquoise in its shorewise shallows. The blue becomes darker, almost indigo, as we press seawards. The day is beautiful and the temperature now, within our little four-man planet one thousand feet aloft, is bland. The Maryland is purring along and all the dials are showing satisfactory norms.

There is a click in my ears and I hear the harsh 'shurr-r-r' of an open microphone. Dutton calls: 'Just going to test my guns, skipper!'

'Okay.' It is a succinct, bastard of a word — multi-lingual and multi-usable, whatever the acknowledgement. 'You, too, Mike — you try 'em out.'

'Wilco,' says Mike Conway. That is another bit of butchered English spawned by the wise signals men of Allied Combined Services. It means that Mike will co-operate.

There is the sound of clattering from behind the bulkhead of my cockpit and a tremor of vibration. I check the trim of the aircraft slightly as the two men swap places in the turret, and Conway tries his hand at the twin Brownings that Dutton has just tested.

A noise still offends my ears. 'Shur-r-r-r. . .'

'Who's bloody mike is still left on?'

The din ceases with a click. All are blameless.

Our estimated time of arrival on this compass heading is 1100 hours. Sergeant Hall has taken drift sightings and assessed the effects of wind on our track. The correction to our course is but minimal. I give myself to the Coastal Command pilot's lot. I groan from buttock to buttock, my tortured hams seeking relief from the bumps and knobs of the inflatable dinghy in the seat-pack of my parachute. I search the wave tops and the hazy horizon and the bright blue sky. I watch each dial and each trembling little finger of fate that tells of petrol used and speed maintained; and of pressures and of therms. And I listen. Ah, yes — I listen for the sour notes that may come from my engines with a far keener ear than any maestro may cock towards his sighing strings or his sounding brass.

Why, on this smiling Mediterranean morning, am I here? A good question. Why is Dutton, my county cricketer comrade in arms, here? And taciturn Hall and freckled-faced Conway? It is, perhaps, an opportune time to ponder philosophy. I have been told that I am fighting for a free world. I have not denied this, any more than I have fervently seized on this as my cause. But, probably more to the point is the fact that I am trying to prove something. A gauntlet has been thrown down and I have dared to pick it up and meet the challenge.

Dutton, I am sure, treats this as a match away from the home field. The red-white-and-blue Roundels team is playing the red-white-and-black Swastikas. After the game, if Ces Dutton does not get clobbered by a body-line ball, there will be tea and buns for both teams in the pavilion.

Why are you here, quiet Sergeant Hall? And you, Mike Conway — all the way from Toronto — what is your business over Mare Nostrum waters?

One might as well ask the ghosts of Ulysses's men, or the shades of old Phoenecians, why they went marauding across the Mediterranean Sea.

I look at my watch. We are nearing the ETA. But, as yet, there is no sign of the enemy. I consult Sergeant Hall about our search of the sea. He has been busy on the preparations of such an exercise and we proceed as planned on what we call an extended-Y search. We are to zig-zag our way forward. Every parallel leg of our track becoming longer as we comb a big, broad 'Y' of the sea.

We have flown but two legs of the search when I see a smudge of smoke within the distant haze. 'There it is — the convoy! There, at one o'clock!'

I take the Maryland down to about fifty feet off the surface of the sea and we run in on our quarry. I call to my gunners, quite needlessly, to watch for enemy aircraft cover. The Axis convoys are under a continuous umbrella of Ju-88 guardianship from Grecian and Cretan airfields until they are out of the range of their aerial protectors and informants.

We close the distance, Hall and I peering ahead to see how many enemy ships we have fossicked out of the sea, Dutton standing by his wireless key to send base our findings, and Conway squatting in his turret, his fingers on the triggers of his twin Brownings.

There are three — four — five largish merchantmen plodding their way southward under the escort of two destroyers. Hall and I compare notes on the ships' size, course and speed. Dutton gets our information and begins coding his message. I turn away from the flotilla and, retreating, begin to climb so that our wireless signal will carry strongly across the miles of sea that divide us from base.

'Skipper! Bogey — bogey right behind! Range half a mile!' Conway has sighted trouble. We are being chased by an enemy convoy-escort aircraft.

I dive for the wave tops again.

'He's on your port now, skipper. Closing in. Range three hundred yards. Turning on us, now. Closing in. . . closing. Start your turn to port. . . *now*!'

I turn the aircraft in towards the attacker, tightening up his curve of pursuit. From the corner of my eye I see a flurry of white water away to my right. It is like a school of giant trevalli shoaling in Bay of Islands waters. But I know that no fish have made this disturbance.

There is a staccato racket coming from aft and the Maryland judders. A pungent rasp of cordite bites my nostrils.

'Did you get the bastard, Mike?'

'Nah!' Conway growls his disappointment into the microphone.

'Where now?'

The Ju-88, overshooting us, is now poised for an attack from our starboard quarter. Mike Conway is on his commentary again: 'Coming in now. Three hundred yards. Weave, skipper, weave. Get ready to turn right — turn right. . . *now*!'

Again the bedlam from the turret and the smell of cordite. And again the thrashed water where the enemy's fire went wide.

'Christ, you nearly dug your starb'd wingtip into the sea, then, boss,' Conway calls.

'Where now?' I demand. 'Is he still after us?'

'He's broken off now, skipper. He's buggered off back to his bloody boats.'

'Ships!' Hall chides.

I am holding the Maryland down as hard as I can. It has a determination to rise. I let it come up to about two hundred feet above sea level and then I throttle back. But still the aircraft is climbing. I check the elevator trim wheel; but it is at normal setting.

I call to Conway: 'Say — look at my elevators and see if they are okay. The bloody kite is climbing and I've got to fight like hell to keep the nose down.'

'The tail is a bit tatty. Looks as though that Jerry bastard might have put a shot or two through it.'

'He's wrecked the elevator servo tabs, I reckon.'

Then I check with Ces Dutton's department. Yes, he has tapped out his first sighting signal, so that base will now know that we've come up on the convoy and can now digest the information.

I ask Hall to unship the folded auxiliary control stick in the navigator's compartment and give me a hand to bear down on the aircraft's dedication to soar heavenwards.

He grumbles in his confusion. He has his navigational sums to complete first. Then he gives me a course for home. He unfolds the emergency 'deadman' control column and the two of us lean on our hand-wheels all the weary nautical miles back to Gianaclis.

Maryland crew after a Mediterranean sortie.

9

Warburton's Domain

By October 1942, 203 Squadron was well on the way to being equipped with Baltimore light bombers, which were American aircraft built by Glenn Martin. They were modifications of and, allegedly, improvements on the Marylands we had been using.

They were chunkier aeroplanes than their predecessors and they still retained the droop-gutted fuselage underlines, but more so. They were powered by Wright Cyclone engines and, like the Marylands, they maintained complete segregation of pilot from navigator, and navigator from the two WOP-AGs. Once aboard the machine, the only communication between the three compartments was by intercom.

Both the Maryland and the Baltimore gave no joy whatsoever to the unlucky navigator in the event of a ditching. The poor fellow was imprisoned within his transparent-nose compartment with an excellent view of oncoming disaster. A solid bulkhead behind him denied any hope of retreat from the inrush of water when the aircraft hit the water.

I went off solo in a Baltimore after one circuit as a passenger sitting in the navigator's compartment. Then, having taken it off and landed it safely on my own, I flew the machine for a further thirty-five minutes, exploring the various knobs and switches and was then considered fit to take my crew on an operational anti-submarine patrol to Port Said. Our conversion to Baltimore flying was, one might say, of pressure-cooking urgency.

After one more patrol our aircraft, along with two others, took off for Malta to augment 69 Squadron's thin ranks. Ces Dutton was still my senior WOP-AG. His companion in the dorsal turret was Sergeant Dorsey and our new navigator, replacing Les Norman and the stop-gap crew member, Sergeant Hall, was Sergeant Swinfield.

Snibbo Baum and his crew mates had earlier flown their Baltimore to Malta — or, to be precise, had flown towards that island. But he didn't arrive. When I heard the news I wrote to his pretty Kath and, while expressing my sorrow, gave old Snibbo such a grand eulogy as he, in his Valhalla, would hardly have believed, had he peeped down over my shoulder as I wrote.

But, of course, the bugger didn't perish. A week or two after his disappearance I had a letter from Kath, buoyant with relief and love of life, saying that her Frank (she had never heard him called by any other name) had been shot down by a German aircraft, had ditched his machine and had managed to take to his inflatable dinghy, and had been picked up by an Italian ship bound for Taranto. He had not been badly injured and at Kath's time of writing he was a prisoner of war in Italy. His navigator, Taffy Davies, had unfortunately suffered a broken back and there had been no news of Willie Williams, Snibbo's WOP-AG.

Number 69 Squadron, under the command of the redoubtable and flamboyant Wing Commander Adrian Warburton, had suffered heavy losses, particularly in 'A' Flight where Baltimores played the unit's daylight reconnaissance role, and Squadron Leader Mac McKay, the flight commander, was understandably glad of reinforcements.

Mac had come up smartly on the ladder of promotion. Only six months earlier he had been a sergeant, but no sooner had he been commissioned in the rank of acting pilot officer than he found himself elevated to the rank of acting flying officer. He did not remain long at this level. Many casualties within the Baltimore flight meant that someone on the spot had to take over leadership duties immediately. Ergo, McKay, who had yet to serve the required probationary period before he could become a substantive pilot officer, found himself wearing the braid of a squadron leader.

Acting Squadron Leader McKay was an Australian. He and I got along very well from the outset, considering that I was then only a flight-sergeant. But, as Mac himself pointed out, he was really only an acting pilot officer still on probation.

The squadron was based at Luqa. It was a hard-worked and remarkable unit, renowned for its triple role as a photo-reconnaissance, daylight-reconnaissance and strike force. It had been born of a small unit of four aircraft known as Flight 431 in September 1940. Its machines were three Marylands and a Blackburn Skua. Adrian Warburton, who was then a pilot officer with a GR (General Reconnaissance) rating, had been assigned to navigate one of the Marylands from Gibraltar to Malta.

From the time he first set foot on the island, this strange, aloof young man found something that he had not known in his native England. He was enrolled in the flight and forthwith began to navigate on daylight reconnaissance missions with the one or two pilots of the small unit. Within a week he was piloting a Maryland and after the second week he was flying the machine on operational sorties.

Warburton had joined the RAF before the war on a short-service commission. But, as some who knew him say, he was considered no great shakes as a pilot; and his private life, it seems, also had its complications. So the wing commander of the Blackburn Botha squadron in which Warburton served was happy enough to nominate the rather wild young officer for posting to the Mediterranean.

A month after he had been with Flight 431, Pilot Officer Warburton shot down an Italian seaplane with the wing Browning of his Maryland. He had now been blooded and by now his reconnaissance flights were taking him far over the Mediterranean, and well into Sicilian and Italian territory. As well as his cameras, he carried bombs and machine-gun armaments. On Christmas Eve 1940 he brought down an Italian Sm-79 near Naples.

Early in 1941, Flight 431 was elevated to the status of 69 Squadron and, besides its Marylands, it now had two or three Hurricane fighters on its strength. And Warburton was soon to become the squadron's commanding officer.

When the supply of Maryland light bombers dried up, the squadron was re-equipped with Baltimore aircraft, despite Warburton's initial distaste for the machines. He had, at the time, taken a fancy to the Bristol Beaufighter, claiming it to be the fastest aeroplane in the Mediterranean. Using one of these lively British twin-engined fighters as an example, he had persuaded the then Air Officer Commanding Malta, Air Vice-Marshal H P Lloyd that he had a superb vehicle for photo-reconnaissance work.

'With this Beaufighter,' Warburton told the AOC, 'I can reconnoitre any place at any height and at any time. And I can bring you back some damn good photos, too.'

'Right,' said Air Vice-Marshal Lloyd. 'If you are so happy with the aircraft, get me all the photographs you can of all the ports and airfields of Sicily.'

Within a couple of days Warburton had taken a series of clear photographs to provide a selection that the AOC had wanted for some time. He had flown at the particularly vulnerable height of six thousand feet on most of the sorties; but on one particular occasion he had come in low enough to get himself involved in the circuit pattern over one of the enemy airfields.

For good measure he set out on the following day and photographed all the airfields of Tripolitania.

He charmed women and inspired his fellow officers and his groundstaff. No stickler for conformity, he would swagger around the airfield in a crumpled khaki uniform with his long blond hair waving from below a villainous, scruffy cap. Always ready to assist in the servicing of his beloved Beaufighter, he would peel off his tunic and go to the aid of his fitters and riggers.

Wg Cmdr Adrian Warburton, DSO and Bar, DFC and 2 Bars.

He charmed the gods of war, too. Throughout his service life on Malta he was unharmed, although hotly pursued on many occasions, by the enemy. He stripped his aircraft of armaments in the interests of lightness when he became wholly committed to photo-reconnaissance work. And he did not carry a regular crew of a qualified navigator or WOP-AG. Two members of his groundstaff, however, were frequent passengers on Warburton's flights over enemy territory. They were Leading Aircraftman Shirley and Aircraftman 2nd Class Haddon and they attended to the loading and unloading of the cameras.

The aircraftmen were not supposed to fly. They had no 'trade' qualifications for this line of duty. But Warburton and his men did many things they were not supposed to do. And it was typical of their guide and mentor that he made sure that both Shirley and Haddon were awarded the Distinguished Flying Medal, notwithstanding that they were not strictly aircrew.

Warburton himself was to go on and win the Distinguished Service Order with Bar and the Distinguished Flying Cross with two Bars.

When his beloved Beaufighter was wrecked on the ground by enemy bombing, he took command of a Spitfire and, as with his earlier photo-reconnaissance machine, it was stripped of all unnecessary weight in the interests of extra height and speed. Armour plating and machine guns were considered excess baggage. The cameras were all important. And as the Spitfire was essentially a single-seater, there was no room for helpers like Shirley and Haddon.

It was while flying this Spitfire over the Mediterranean that Warburton was shot down for the first time. But he was able to glide to the mainland of Tunisia, then happily in the hands of the Allies, and land safely. Transported to Gibraltar, he commandeered another Spitfire and vengefully returned to the area of Tunisia where he had been so embarrassingly 'downed'. Somewhere near the spot where his aircraft had crashed, he destroyed a German Ju-88 and damaged another in an aerial scrap.

Three or four days later, after being posted missing on RAF records, he arrived back at Luqa. He proceeded to tear the heavy armament out of his new Spitfire and was soon back on his photographic sorties. In the meantime 69 Squadron had grown in stature and reputation; and with its commanding officer now a wing commander, orders came from the new AOC Malta, Air Vice-Marshal Sir Keith Park, requiring Warburton to curb his operational sorties and devote more time to the ground duties of administration. This he did to a degree, but he still climbed into his Spitfire at the drop of a bomb to hare off into the blue sky to click his camera shutters.

With more than five hundred operational sorties in his log book, he was to survive the turbulent sieges of Malta, only to disappear while flying with the United States Air Force some time after the heavy pressure of aerial bombing was removed from the small fortress island that Warburton practically claimed as his own arena.

Some pilots have said that Warburton was a natural flyer. I do not believe he was. To say that he was such would be simplifying his deeds. He came to Malta under some cloud of official disapproval, a pilot (as some who knew him intimately could say) with only 'average' or even, sometimes, 'below average' flying assessments in his log-book, yet who was to later write up a record five hundred or more operational sorties. He was an iconoclast, an individualist, and extrovert. He was a man with something to prove. And Malta was the place where he could do it. Came the hour, the place and the man.

The day I first saw my new CO of 69 Squadron, Wing Commander Warburton was wearing a scraped and greasy Irvin jacket over his khaki battle dress. A pair of fantastic, thigh-length black-and-white goat-skin leggings were added protection against high-altitude cold and, tucked under a leather thong lashed around his left calf like a garter, was a German two-edged dagger — flogged originally, I suspect, from some Teutonic corpse on Crete.

He nodded to me pleasantly enough when Mac McKay introduced us. But he did not bother to ask any details of me. I was now here on Malta and, specifically, in his squadron. Whether I liked it or not was apparently of no great concern to him. Pilots and their crews came — and they went. That was the war we were fighting.

However, I was soon to find that my CO was, in fact, a very human fellow. The second day after our arrival at Luqa we flew an operational patrol off the south coast of Sicily, and as far north-west as Sardinia. The expectation was that we might see some enemy shipping coming down from Italy. We were at a higher than usual altitude for our type of work — about 12,000 feet — and although we did not see anything of significance on the water, we did meet an enemy fighter aircraft face to face. We had been weaving through high columns of cumulo-nimbus, as white and as seemingly solid as carved marble monuments, when this ugly machine flashed past less than fifty yards distant from us. Doubtless, he was as surprised as we were, and if he had been of an adventurous turn of mind he could have turned and pursued us. Our twin Brownings in the old Mark I Baltimore would have been no match for his front armour.

The next day we were searching for ships of the Italian fleet east of Malta and again we returned a nil report. The early part of November 1942 had been quiet, but on the sixth day of that month Beaufighters of 272 Squadron and Wellingtons of 104 Squadron, Egypt, suddenly made their appearance on Malta. We learned the reason soon enough. The British and American invasion of Algeria and Morocco, which move the Axis forces saw as a threat to their advantages in Tunisia, meant that all available German and Italian aircraft from Sicily were being diverted to this new front. So our Beaufighter and Wellington visitors on Malta were here in an offensive rather than a defensive role.

The Allies' 'Operation Torch' was in train, and this involved a three-pronged landing of troops. The Americans would go in at Casablanca and at Oran. The British would attack Algiers, further east and nearer to Axis territories. And it was to Algiers that the two squadrons, 272 and 104, would fly on their strike missions.

Meanwhile, 69 Squadron was flying continuous reconnaissance patrols. We searched in vain for the Italian fleet which, reason told us, should be showing itself in a bid to help the Axis defenders of Tunisia. But on 5 December we had a field day, sending in six sighting reports of wheeling, foam-churning destroyers far below us. Their ack-ack fire was thick but somewhat awry as we continued to weave and bash out our amplifying wireless messages.

But we stayed on the job a bit too long. On our turning towards base I saw with concern that my petrol gauges were indicating a hefty petrol consumption that somehow did not match with our flight-plan estimates. And as we plodded the weary nautical miles I sweated over the cold, impersonal dials and the twitching, sagging needles. I kept looking at my wrist-watch as we droned over the landless sea and was but faintly heartened to hear from my navigator that we were right on course. Our estimated time of arrival was forever an eternity away, it seemed.

At last the grey coastline of Malta came into view and by now the petrol gauges were showing our fuel supply as practically nil. The port motor cut out, coughed into life for a reassuring minute or two and then died. We came over the edge of the island and I began to search helplessly for a spot on which I could belly-flop the Baltimore within the maze of tiny, stone-walled fields that is the countryside of Malta.

I had by now given the starboard motor all the throttle I could to keep the aircraft flying. And by this time it, too, was beginning to falter. Luqa airfield was now but a matter of a mile away — and I was heading straight into wind. I came reaching for the runway on my one spluttering starboard motor and even as I was positioning to let down my gear, the last few pints of fuel were consumed. The Baltimore came rushing earthwards with the gliding angle of a brick. It fell out of my hands, powerless, and crashed almost on the downwind end of the runway.

The four of us emerged bruised and shaken. I could barely walk with the terrible pain in my pelvis.

Warburton came on the scene in some concern. He had a bent Baltimore, which would not help Malta's contribution to the war effort. And he wanted to assess the condition of the manpower that had emerged from the shambles. He looked us over and he saw me, the only one with outward signs of injury, limping considerably before I sagged down in a near faint.

'What's the matter, Sanders?' he asked. 'What have you done to yourself?'

I told him I had hurt myself here, and I pointed to an area roughly between my genitals and my right hip bone. I moaned: 'Christ, someone's going to get killed in this bloody war, someday!'

My admirable commanding officer, who had experienced a bit of bother with Bothas himself in the not-so-dim past, grinned: 'Yes, that just could be so right.'

'I'm bloody sorry, sir,' I muttered as I looked at the wrecked aircraft.

'Don't be a prick,' said Warburton.

I was shepherded away to the medical officer, who prescribed a day or two respite from flying.

The groundcrew boys found there was a faulty valve connected to the wing tanks. My aircraft's belly tank had been flown dry, as was our practice, before I had switched over to my wing tanks. But owing to the leaking valve, a lot of wing tank petrol had drained back into the belly tank, giving indications of excessive petrol consumption.

10
A Maltese Soliloquy

I sit outside 'A' Flight office in the thin sunshine of a Maltese winter's morning. The day is clear and the wide inverted dome of the sky is free of cloud from the hostile strands of Sicily to the shores of Tripoli. The only object that intrudes on the serenity of the heavens in this rare, peaceful fragment of time is a tiny white petal of parachute silk that seems to be taking an interminable time to lower its pendant RAF fight pilot towards the offshore waters.

We off-duty loungers look upwards from time to time, speculating on the parachutist's frame of mind as he drifts 'twixt welkin and waves. Knowing that the island's Air-Sea Rescue launch will be puttering around waiting to receive its cargo from the blue, we are not greatly concerned with the fellow's welfare now that he is free from his crippled aircraft. He is alive — or he was, certainly, when he 'hit the silk' — and there, but for the grace of God . . .

I am indulging my artistic talents in our latest whimsy — the carving of chunks of the local white sandstone into fanciful shapes and statuary. Some of the fellows have fashioned, with sharp bits of iron and penknives, lewd nudes and crude busts, none of which would push Michelangelo's work into the background. My effort of the moment is the creation of a relief plaque badge for 69 Squadron. Within the standard laurel wreath of the device I am chiselling with a screwdriver is a hawk volant before a Maltese cross. The bird carries a Naval telescope in its claws.

Sonny Cliffe and Andy Covich, two fellow New Zealanders who are WOP-AGs in 'A' Flight, are watching me.

'What does it mean?' asks Sonny. 'What's that bird thing that you've got there?'

'It's a bloody hawk — a *sea* hawk, see — with this telescope in his fist. He's a super-snooper, see, and he's flying over Malta. The squadron was formed in Malta and its job is reconnaissance in co-operation with the Navy.'

'Not bad!' admires Andy. 'Not bad at all. Has Warby seen it? I reckon he'd like it.'

'Yes, he's seen it. He wants me to draw a picture of it, too, so he can send it off to England. He'd like to get something like it approved as the squadron badge.'

'What's your motto going to be? A badge has got to have a motto,' states Sonny.

'I've thought of that, too. I reckon "With Vigilance We Serve" would be a good one.'

'He's coming close, now,' says Andy.

'Warby?'

'No, dumbo, the poor sod with the parachute.'

'And a bloody sight poorer without it he'd be,' Sonny speculated.

We look across the Luqa skyline of bomb-snaggled masonry to see that the fighter pilot, by the kindness of the Almighty and through the excellence of Mr Irvin's safety device, is now nearing his ducking.

'Another candidate for the Caterpillar Club,' says Sonny. 'Another one lives to fly again.'

'I hope he can swim,' says Andy. 'I hope the launch is standing by to collect him.'

'It's had long enough time to get out there,' I observe. 'The fellow's come down from, what? Twenty thousand feet? Old Dut will be there to look after him.'

Dutton, my erstwhile WOP-AG, is now doing a rest stint as a gunner on the Air-Sea Rescue launch. I now have an Australian navigator, Flight-Sergeant Thorpe, and Sonny and Andy as WOP-AGs to complete my crew. While I was in hospital, Swinfield and Dorsey went their separate ways to other crews, as casualties made necessary.

We are to be airborne by 1000 hours. Our patrol will be what we call the 'Messina Block', a watching brief on any shipping that may be coming through the Strait of Messina that separates Sicily from the toe of Italy. The area is well defended by Axis fighter aircraft and we will be in plain sight throughout the sortie.

The day is Wednesday 23 December in this year of our Lord, 1942. The sky is blue — too blue and too clear of clouds for the likings of this crew. And it is my forty-second operational trip. Our aircraft is Baltimore AG755 — B-Baker.

We are briefed. We know the bounds of our search area and we have our signal codes and our identification colours of the day contained in Very cartridges in the racks of the aircraft. Our inflatable dinghy packs are fastened to our parachutes and we have divested our pockets of any give-away snippets of information, should we be shot down and captured, alive or dead, by the enemy.

Those of us who have not already devoured them out of sheer hunger still carry a few malted milk tablets, along with pep pills and silk escape-route maps, in our emergency packs. And each of us has, disguised as one of the fly buttons in our trousers, a magnetic compass that will give us a rough north reading when suspended on a thread.

Burdened with the accoutrements of flight, we clump our ways to B-Baker, which is sheltering in its three-sided revetment, and there is the interminable adjusting and testing of equipment before the engines are ready to be started and run up. But at last we have power in both engines and we are moving gingerly out of the protective dispersal bay and edging along the perimeter towards the take-off end of the runway.

'Don't try a "Paddy Martin" on us, will you!' Thorpe quips.

'Not bloody likely.'

Paddy Martin, a transient pilot marooned on Malta, is one of the school who sports a pukka RAF handlebar moustache, battered cap and garish scarf. He had admired the antics of one of the Hurricane pilots whose habit was to tear his machine along the runway on take-off, reach flying speed, and whip up his undercarriage without raising his aircraft an inch until he neared the end of the strip.

'Bloody fascinating!' Paddy had breathed. 'I'm going to try that.'

On his next air-test flight, Paddy gunned the ageing Hurricane along the runway, reckoned the big moment had arrived, and pulled up his gear.

T-wang! It takes a steady hand, a lot of throttle and some fine engine tuning to keep an aircraft stable at such a critical height with the tips of the propeller so dangerously close to the ground. Paddy

Martin managed to stagger his machine off the deck in a cloud of sparks and dust and pulverized asphalt to complete a perilous circuit. The Hurricane had sagged at the moment of Paddy's removing its fourth dimension. The airscrew tips had thrashed the runway and abrazed about four inches off each of the three blades. Unbalanced and alarmed, the valiant Rolls-Royce Merlin engine had taken the shock, picked up the beat, revved a bit harder and brought Flying Officer Martin safely home.

No, I would not be trying a 'Paddy Martin' take-off.

We roar down the runway. And when I feel the Baltimore's responses, I ease back on the column and the machine takes to the air. As the maintenance buildings and the revetment bays fall away below us I take up the undercarriage and let off the small amount of flap I have used to get us airborne quickly. I pull back some of the power and, having checked all the gauges to my satisfaction, I proceed to climb B-Baker, spiralling up over Luqa until we are at two thousand feet. And then I set course on Thorpie's direction and we move northwards into hostile territory.

We throb upwards. Below us, like a leaf floating on the blue sea, Malta spreads out flat and grey. Under our port wing now, lies the Great Harbour of Valletta. Beyond, away to the north-west, lies the ancillary island of Gozo.

I shift my weight beneath the restricting harness of my safety straps, seeking relief from pressure. My pelvis is abominably sore since my last ill-starred flight which ended in a crash at the end of the runway. I have been rested since, shuffling my ways between our dormitory in the Poor House, the sergeants' mess and the flight office at Luqa airfield. And I had spent ten days in the island's service hospital, suffering from food poisoning.

'*Food* poisoning?' Sonny had quipped when he visited me. 'Where did you get any food to be poisoned with, anyhow?'

My weight is about twenty pounds lighter than it was when I left New Zealand eighteen months ago. My mouth is dry and foul-tasting. My eyes are sunken and they peer out from under brows that overhang my field of vision. I can feel the wrinkled flesh above the sockets folding in and pressing on my eye-balls. Sometimes I have double vision. I am ill.

Now I can see Malta, lying drab and melancholy seven thousand feet below us. Oh yes, I can indeed see Malta. And I can feel it, even at this height. I can, in fact, almost smell the putrefaction of death that haunts the place, rising up through the thin cold air, blending with the odours of acetate, petrol, plastic, oil, rubber and sweat that marinate the inside of this duralumin capsule holding us between wind and water.

Death and the cockpit. To me, at 1030 hours on this clear, crisp morning so close to Christmas, their odours are synonymous.

Malta, the 'Holy Island' that the British had occupied since 1800, is a sliver of land seventeen miles long and nine miles wide. Before this war there were about one and a quarter million people living on its ninety-five square miles of soil-sparse land. It lies sixty miles from the south coast of Sicily and about one hundred and eighty miles from North Africa. It is predominately flat to undulating and its highest hill is no more than eight hundred feet above sea level. Churchill has called it our unsinkable aircraft carrier. We have other names for it.

But we fly out on every call that is made of us to ensure the goddamn slab of mudstone is held secure in the name of the British Crown. I lie if I say I get airborne with eagerness and patriotic fervour. But I die, I know — spiritually and morally — if ever I am moved to beg excuse from my duty.

This island, our vital watch post and our gun platform in the Mediterranean Sea, has been a citadel and a haven for other races in other wars since man first shambled across the earth. It was believed for a long time that the first colonists of Malta were the Phoenicians, but since the discovery of neolithic temples on the island, this notion, often repeated, does not stand up against tangible proofs. The presence of large megalithic buildings, dating back to 3000 BC, testifies to the existence of earlier civilizations than the Phoenicians, who colonized the Western Mediterranean no earlier than 1500 BC.

During the Punic Wars of 250 BC, Malta was many times pillaged by the Romans, and in the year AD 58 the ship conveying the prisoner St. Paul was wrecked on the Maltese shore. That Christian, accompanied by St. Luke, remained on the island for about three months, performing his miracles and converting the Maltese to Christianity.

The island came under Saracenic rule and it was later annexed to Sicily. The Knights of St. John took over administration in 1530, until Napoleon seized the small land in 1798. He held it but briefly. The Maltese petitioned England for help and Sir Alexander Ball was sent to preside in 1800.

Ah, yes. Malta has a history. It has seen many changes over

thousands of years, and it has had many defenders. So it is fair enough, I suppose, that now on this clear morning in December 1942, three New Zealanders and one Australian should be climbing high in the air above this coveted clod, adding our modest contributions to the island's hoary annals.

But what is this? A red warning light flashes on the panel in front of me. It is silent, but its muteness screams, *'Watch it, pilot — your petrol is low!'*

How can that be? It is a lying little bulb — I hope. We have been airborne less than thirty minutes and the trembling fingers on my fuel gauges point reassuringly to the word 'Full' on each dial. I lean forward and thump the instrument panel with my fist as I would strike an ageing, crackling radio set. But the red light still shines.

I call to the boys in the turret behind me for assurance. 'We are not losing petrol, are we? You don't see any petrol streaming out?' And I should have added '. . . I hope.'

No, they report, all is clear behind. But my inquiry has triggered concern among them. 'What is the trouble, skipper?' Andy asks.

'It's this petrol warning light. It's just come on. But the gauges are reading full.'

Uneasily, we make conjecture and then agree that here is a job for the instrument bashers when we get back to base. Apparently we have a faulty electrical connection. But after my last escapade with the malfunctioning petrol cocks, I have my doubts. It is very disconcerting.

The morning that had been so disturbingly clear is now presenting us with a few fluffy clouds. As a child I had always imagined that these vapour masses were blown into my field of vision from somewhere beyond the north, south, east or west horizon. I now know that they form as they fancy, whenever and wherever the aerial conditions allow. They breed prolifically.

Now these white, woolly clumps of mist could not have happened at a better time or a better place. We are stooging northwards towards Sicily and the hazy, dun-coloured land mass of that country is below our port wingtip.

'Thank Christ for cloud cover,' says Thorpie, reading my mind.

'We're going to need it,' Sonny calls from the dorsal turret. 'There's a couple of fighters climbing up towards us.'

The adrenalin is working in my juices. My senses are tingling and my hide is goosefleshed. I am keenly alert for Sonny's evasion-action commentary and ready to dive, turn and weave as he may direct.

The author's Blenheim navigator, Sergeant Les Norman, sights a bearing from his rather cramped nose compartment. Western Desert, 1942.

A Glenn Martin Maryland of 203 Squadron. Western Desert, 1942.

The author at the controls of an Avro Anson, Squires Gate, 1943.

Sergeants swarming on Blenheim A-Apple at Fuka, Western Desert, in 1942. The author's navigator, Les Norman, and WOP-AG, Ces Dutton, are sitting left. Sgt-Pilot Snibbo Baum sits on the turret with his navigator, Taffy Davis, to his right. Standing is Baum's WOP-AG, Willie Williams.

A dead Luftwaffe pilot lies atop the wreckage of his burning Junkers-88 fighter-bomber, shot down over Malta.

The Glenn Martin Maryland Mk I. Used extensively in the Western Desert and on Malta as both a light bomber and a nimble reconnaissance aircraft.

The author and his Blenheim crew on leave at Alexandria. From left: Ces Dutton, the author and Les Norman.

A Luftwaffe bomb exploding close to a Vickers Wellington at Luqa airfield, Malta, circa 1942.

'Keep your eyes on them,' I say needlessly. 'Where are they now?'

'Eight o'clock down — down about a thousand feet. But climbing fast in a loose pair.'

Sonny's little word picture is crystal clear. We use the clockface system for the ready location of anything in the sky. Twelve o'clock is straight ahead of the aircraft's nose. Six o'clock is dead astern.

I am looking at God's gift of cloud cover to harried airmen. The patches extend from several hundred feet below us, where they are but little wisps, to nicely bunched masses well into the heavens above. I ease the stick back and gun the engines. The Baltimore bellows as it climbs. I am taking us into safer territory where we may play tag amongst the alto-cumulus.

'Closing on us fast,' snaps Sonny. 'They'll be after our belly. Get ready to turn left skipper. Get ready — ready — *now!*'

My turn to port has given Sonny's twin Brownings a clear field of fire. There is the familiar juddering coming from behind my cockpit's bulkhead and the sharp tang of cordite wafts through.

'Tracer! Look at it!' Thorpe yells from his forward glasshouse. He must be wishing vainly for a shield of armour-plate steel.

Thump! The Baltimore's port air-intake manifold has been partly torn from its anchoring rivets and is leaning forward at a crazy angle. The engine below it misses a few beats and then decides to carry on its lawful rhythm. Somewhere in its complexity of cylinder-pots and wires and tubes it is harbouring a spent missile. I hope the hunk of lead has done no more than wreck the air manifold. I fervently pray that it is not an incendiary bullet or that it has not bared electric leads so as to make a fire hazard in the motor.

Fire? Sweet Jesus, not that, please! Elijah may be the patron saint of aviators, but we don't want to go to Heaven in a chariot of fire! We still have plenty of petrol. As I look down between the exposed longerons in my cockpit floor I can see an area of the yellow auxiliary fuel tank that occupies the aircraft's bomb bay. It holds many, many gallons of petrol, the stuff that the Royal Flying Corps pilots used to call devil juice, witches' water and orange death. How easily the stuff could ignite. How agonizingly long would be the few seconds of our incineration.

But the port engine continues to pound out its horsepower with no further outward sign of complaint. And the little red light, forgotten in the first flurry of excitement, has decided to extinguish itself.

We have plunged into a cloud; and my eyes are on the instruments now, watching the behaviour of the miniature aeroplane datum shape on the artificial horizon dial. It represents our own aircraft's position, obeying every movement of climb, descent and turn that I ask of the Baltimore through my hands and my feet. It is my guide against spatial disorientation. Wherever that little aircraft shape is in relation to the dial's horizon, so is our actual aeroplane aligned with the actual rim of the earth.

My gyro compass, which I have manually mated to my magnetic instrument, shows me that I am holding course. Engine revolutions and boost readings are normal.

My world has gone white. Nothing shows through the curved windscreen and side panels of my little cabin in the sky but a snowy mass of water particles. This is very good — unless there is a long-odds event of our colliding with one of the enemy aircraft. It must be a very long cloud; or the few seconds that we have been in it must be dragging like minutes. Then suddenly — Flash! We are in bright sunshine and four pairs of eyes are raking the skies.

'Do you see 'em?' I ask.

'N-o-o-o,' deliberates Sonny. And then: 'Yes, yes! Look, over at nine o'clock, level, about three hundred yards!'

One of the fighters from Syracuse has just appeared from behind a cloud. It is an Me-109. The pilot see us and banks sharply towards us. He has lost his mate in the clouds but is determined on a solo attack.

Again there comes the juddering and the acrid whiff of cordite. But before we can assess results I have found the harbour of a cloud and we are once more engulfed in heavy fog. We proceed towards the Strait of Messina to take up our patrol. Our aggressors have gone.

Back and forth, forth and back we cruise, but not a ship shows. So, towards the end of our petrol endurance, we pack up and Thorpie gives me a course for base.

We are flying over a vast plain of white cloud tops. Our mission completed, we have climbed to avoid the interferences of any more enemy fighters. A hundred feet below us the strata stretches out like a wide snowscape. I am thin and weary and ill. And perhaps I am having illusions — seeing mirages? We are lonely explorers in the thin, aerial wastes. We are a million miles from earth and the shabby politics of earthlings. We fly outside of ourselves and watch, from a strange remoteness that may be the Hereafter, the movements of these husks that are our flesh and bodies inside this machine. A certain nobility is invested in us, perhaps because we are so close to Heaven.

The westing sun peeps out from behind a veil and catches the billows of the clouds with gold, painting them with heart-clutching beauty. My God, if you are up there I am closer to you this instant than ever before. If I have harvested nothing more than this moment from my humble history of flight, I am fortunate indeed. My hands hold the control-column grips of our aerial craft, our little island in the sky, and I steer the destinies of four antipodeans who are a long way from home. I am winging our way back to safety so that we may fly another day. I am Apollo bringing back the sun to shine in spring. I am Marco Polo, rich with the findings from Asia. No, the field of cloud stretches out like the cloud wasteland of the Antarctic and I am that great and gallant Englishman, returning distressed and disappointed from the South Pole after the little band has pulled that sledge those hundreds and hundreds of miles.

> '. . . We fought those untoward events with a will and
> conquered. . . the gale howling about us. We are weak,
> writing is difficult, but for my own part I do not regret
> this journey, which has shown that Englishmen can
> endure hardship, help one another, and meet death with
> as great a fortitude as ever in the past. . . We are
> determined still to do our best to the last. . .

Lord, how I want the courage of Captain Robert Falcon Scott!

I ease back the throttles and drop off height. We descend into this magnificent wilderness of white vapour. Wisps of it flash past like smoke from the engine of a speeding express train, just before we enter the mass. We are in the midst of cloud now and the Baltimore bucks and trembles with the hundreds of little turbulences in the saturated, unstable air. All around us is white mystery and again my eyes are glued to my instruments. My angle of glide is moderate, as reported by the little aeroplane sitting just below the demarcation line of the artificial horizon. The altimeter is unwinding steadily, casting off height by hundreds of feet. The boost gauges of each engine are in harmonious accord. The needles of the engine-revolution dials point to normal function. Cylinder-head temperatures are within safety bounds. Petrol reserves are adequate, and the wretched little red light has remained asleep these past several hours.

Now we are out of cloud. Five thousand feet below us, dead ahead, lies Malta. All I have got to do now is run up on the island, drop off height to one thousand feet, shoot my identification colours of the day, lower my gear and land.

We rumble in on the final approach. Down, down. One hand is on the throttles, giving and taking a fraction of an inch to maintain constant airspeed. The other, on the control column hand-grip, checks the nose of the Baltimore and picks up a sagging wing.

Over the end of the runway at ninety miles an hour. Off with power and back with the stick. Back — back. Hold the wheels off — off. . .

Boip! A yelp of anguished rubber as the tyres touch the asphalt and we are down. But all is not right with our landing run. We are listing to port like a ship whose ballast has shifted. I turn my hand-grips hard to starboard, trying to lift the port wing. I am bewildered by the aeroplane's left-side-down attitude. Maybe the oleo leg has collapsed? I am scared. The machine is careering towards the left side of the runway and will crash into a maintenance shed unless I can stay its wayward course. Brakes! Brakes! But not too frantically applied, or we will be over on our nose in flames!

We slither around in a wild and noisy groundloop. There is much dust and exhaust smoke and there is an ominous stench of scorched rubber. We are out of our compartments in double-quick time. None of us has been maimed, but Sonny is nursing a sore head.

Our left tyre has been punctured. In our earlier engagement with the enemy fighters, one of the bullets has bored into the nacelle, hitting the wheel as it reposed in its well.

A Baltimore of 69 Squadron pursued by a Ju-88.

11
Back to Britain

Squadron Leader Mac McKay sent me to see the medical officer and I was again admitted to the military hospital. I was in a pretty ragged state of debility, my eyes seemed out of focus and I was painfully lame. I do not remember much of the early part of my stay in that institution except an enemy bombing of the nearby airfield. But when I had recovered sufficiently to face the various medical examinations, my eyes were irrigated with chemical drops. My lasting memory of that ordeal is that everything went out of focus and I was violently ill over the floor.

I was instructed to peer through an aperture in the end of a long coffin-like box and pull cords in an attempt to line up two sets of movable pegs within the casket. After each manoeuvre I would step back from the peephole with the pathetic eagerness of a child who has tried to spell his name with alphabet building blocks, seeking with wide-eyed innocence the approbation of my examiners.

They did not tell me a thing, but they asked me a lot of questions about my war history and my general health and, in the fullness of time, I was sent back to my billet in the Poor House.

When the report reached him, Mac McKay told me that my eyes were not focusing properly, I was somewhat battered around the pelvic region, I was generally in poor shape and that I would be off flying for a while. Therefore, he reckoned, I had done enough for one tour and that I should go 'on rest' in Egypt.

I protested loudly at that and urged that he should do everything he could to get me posted back to England. So Mac said he would have a talk with Warburton about it. Meanwhile, I was to stick around.

Waiting. The interminable hours of waiting make up about ninety per cent of a serviceman's war. I limped my haggard carcase around the flight office and the small crew room, shamed that I had been removed from the flying roster and feeling as wanted as a cold pork chop on a kosher platter. I listened to the cheery chatter of my flight mates, bursting with post-patrol effervescence, as they came in untying their mae-wests, and I tried to participate in the cross-fire of repartee. But I felt guiltily apart from them. And then one day came information from Warburton's photo-reconnaissance patrols that the Italian fleet was on the move. The Baltimores were needed for a maximum effort shadowing job. All crews were to report in the squadron operations room immediately.

I went along to the briefing. A Canadian flight lieutenant who was contributing to the briefing saw me and good-humouredly asked my reason for being there.

'I want to go along on this trip,' I told him. 'I feel like a bloody loafer, just sitting around the place.'

He shook his head slowly and grinned. And he said the most kindly thing I had every heard from any superior officer in the service. 'Jesus, Sanders — you're the most tryingest pilot I have ever met!' No, he added, I wouldn't be going this time.

I saw the other fellows prepare their flight plans and then depart. And later I saw them all return. All of them, thank God. But for me the war over Mediterranean waters was ended. My fate was, as yet, undecided. Then one morning I heard from a New Zealand pilot who had landed on Malta in transit to the Middle East that Toby Webster was dead. His aircraft had plunged into the sea off the end of the runway at Gibraltar. None of the crew had survived.

Toby had been flying as second-joe in a transport Albemarle. The last time I had seen him was a little more than a year earlier when we had celebrated a short spot of leave together in London. He told me he was doing a great trade in contraband wrist-watches, which he used to strap all the way up his arms under his tunic. He bought them at a good price at Gibraltar and London offered him a nice profit.

I was terribly distressed. We had been very close companions ever since we had first met at Dargaville, back in New Zealand in 1936. We had shared the same boarding house lodgings in that town. And when we found ourselves back in Auckland, our mutual home town, we were together in the same rowing four with the St. George Rowing

Club. We had enlisted in the RNZAF at about the same time and had done our early flying training together.

I sat down and wrote to Toby's mother. But what can mere words say?

It was while I was in this state of wet-eyed melancholia that news came through that an American Air Force DC-3 transport aircraft was due to leave Luqa for Algiers, by way of Maison Blanche.

Mac McKay said to me, 'You'd better get cracking with your gear and get yourself aboard while there's still room — and before the Brass decides to change its mind and shoot you off to Egypt.'

There was quite a crowd of time-expired men aboard the old DC-3. Some were RAF aircrew and some were Canadian pilots and aircrew. But most were American flyers. I was the only New Zealander. The noise chatter was peppered with plenty of 'goddams' and 'gor' blimeys', and the atmosphere within the tight duralumin capsule was redolent of Wrigley's chewing gum and unwashed flesh. All were abundantly pleased that they were leaving Malta, and laughter came easily and a little hysterically to them.

We landed at Maison Blanche, and each managed to grab a mug of coffee before we were on our way again to Algiers — where we spent a week among the inhospitable burghers before we were shipped aboard the *Nea Hellas*, a rather nondescript freighter, and sent off to England.

The ship carried a mixed complement, which one of Robert Louis Stevenson's pirate characters might have called 'a motley crew'. Along with the ship's seamen, a most sullen bunch of fellows, were our lot of airmen from Malta, some soldiers of several of His Majesty's regiments returning from North African affairs, and a bunch of German aircrew prisoners garnered from various ditchings in the Mediterranean and forced landings in the desert.

At sea, day followed day; but nothing untoward disturbed the ship's steady tramp northwards. And then, one bleak morning, a rock showed dimly through the haze on our starboard beam. The Isles of Scilly gave us a silent welcome home. I stood in the cold February air, trying to bore my gaze into the distance, visualizing the land that lay in the mists away to the east. Somewhere in the distance lay Portreath, whence Les Norman, Ces Dutton and I had lumbered into the sky in poor old Blenheim V6257 and headed south on our way to the Middle East.

And further yet in my fond recall I conjured back the rolling lands we had traversed in our many flights from Bicester. Cornwall, Devon, Somerset, Wiltshire, Berkshire, Oxfordshire. . . Dear counties, dear heartland of a country I could well call home.

All day we steamed, pushing up through St. George's Channel into the Irish Sea, cringing from habit from the drone of aircraft, accepting nothing over, on or below the water at its face value until the secret signs and passwords established identity. And on the following morning we slid past the sugarloaf of Ailsa Craig and stood into the Firth of Clyde.

'Ah've stood heah fer ha'f 'n hour or more,' drawled a Canadian warrant officer from his post at the ship's rail, 'an' I ain't heard one gawddamn bagpipe yet.'

We tied up at Greenock, and when we were eventually cleared to disembark, one of the English sergeants, a long time from home, walking down the gangway and stamped his foot on the solidity of Scottish asphalt. He sighed, 'It ain't England yet — but, b'Jesus, it'll bloody well do, in the meantime.'

Soon, we were on the train that was taking us to London.

After reporting at RAF Uxbridge, my early commitments were to get in touch with Ces Dutton's wife, who was living at Chester, and visit Kath Baum. So I phoned Mrs Dutton and told her that Ces was well and, as soon as I could grab a leave pass, I called on young Kathleen. She was as pretty as her photograph and a very warm-hearted girl. She amplified her earlier letter to me by telling of Snibbo's adventures, both before and after his imprisonment. And she took me to visit her parents, who were nearly overcome with pleasurable excitement to know that a friend of Frank should find the time to call.

But, inexorably, time rolls on. I have never heard of Snibbo's home-coming or whatever happened to him and his Kathleen after the war.

Soon after my arrival at Uxbridge, I was called before a panel of examiners from one of the RAF medical boards, and suffered the physical explorations of manicured fingers and the cold, physic probes of cultured tongues. My heart beats were sounded and my blood pressure was measured. My corpuscles, in red and white flights rigidly at attention, tallest on the left, shortest on the right, stood a close inspection. And my urine was analysed. All evidence, so far as I could detect, seemed to indicate that, physically at least, I should be able to gain weight and live in reasonable comfort of the flesh for a while longer. But my scrutineers did not tell me this in so many words.

The RAF psychiatrist, a pale and melancholy flight lieutenant, asked me all manner of questions. Was I ever frightened before a sortie? Did my bowels become over-active before take-off? Was I subject to nightmares? He scowled as he jotted down my responses.

Was I ever frightened? Dear Christ, what did that cheerless, earthbound, clinic-cosseted fellow know of fear and the nervous runs to the latrines before we lumped our parachutes out to the waiting aircraft? What did he know of failing engines and fathomless seas? Was I ever frightened? Jesus, sometimes I was terrified!

But I told him, no. No sir, I said, I didn't get frightened.

Did I like flying?

Beyond the pale, wax-like head of my interrogator was a window. And through the glass that had been reinforced with anti-splinter tape I could see the grey of a London overcast. A couple of barrage balloons, soggy and dully silver, were barely holding up their cables. But somewhere above this starkly efficient room that smelt of tomes and furniture polish, above this cold-fish psychiatrist and the barrage balloons and the depressing clouds, was the boundless blue sky. At this time of the day, late afternoon, the sinking sun would be throwing gold over the crowns of the stratus. And that vast stretch of gilded mistland, the dizzy heights of improbability to this poor mortal sitting opposite me, was but the floor of another world to the flying man.

I said smartly, 'Yes sir. Yes, of course I want to fly.'

He murmured, 'Yes, yes.' And he wrote another of his many notes. Then, after a pause, he smiled a wintery curl of the lips and said, 'That will be fine, flight sergeant. That will be all, thank you.'

A few days later I got my orders and a rail pass. I was to proceed to Squires Gate, Blackpool. I had been posted on rest as a staff pilot of No 3 General Reconnaissance School, where I would be flying Anson trainer aircraft and stooging embryo GR pilots and navigators around the Irish Sea by day and by night.

After a week or two of rest and relief from nervous tension, my eyes were now focusing much better than they had been on Malta, so I found no trouble whatsoever in handling the gentle Anson. We staff pilots took shocking liberties with those old buses and we soon found that they side-slipped beautifully. So, instead of rumbling in over the rooftops of the neighbouring Vickers hangars or shaving the tops of Blackpool's suburban buses as we approached for landings, we would often come in deliberately high, give the machine some left bank and a bit of hard right rudder, and slice off a couple of hundred feet of altitude from a position almost above the approach end of the runway.

A staff pilot and a staff WOP-AG made a two-man team in the trainer Ansons, the pupils (usually two at a time) being more or less supercargoes. We seemed to be always losing trailing aerials, the WOP-AGs' memories failing to remind them to wind in the wretched things before the aircraft landed. And so about sixty yards of hanging wire, weighed at the end by a plumb-bob or 'fish', would wrap itself around a boundary fence or lambaste the chequered flight-control van at the threshold end of the runway.

My regular WOP-AG crew-mate was an Australian boy, Ray Whitney. He, like myself, was a flight sergeant. If we saw the makings of a cold or warm front building up over the Irish Sea, it was a good enough sign that the night flying detail would be cancelled, and that we could soon be cosily entrenched within the downstairs bar of the Casino Hotel — a den known, quite aptly, as the snake pit.

Our RAF-issue bikes would carry us the half-mile from our sergeants' mess in the Southdown Hotel, and a noisy and bibulous hour or two would be spent in the company of our flying companions and other dubious souls. The Middle East and Malta, notwithstanding the shady delights of Cairo or The Gut, were never able to offer the conviviality that Blackpool could provide. Many of the Lancastrians had never heard the explosion of a bomb except in the movie newsreels. The war seemed a million miles away.

Sometimes the frontal clouds that had looked so ominous would disperse with a pattering of drizzle, and a fast and irritable aircraftman runner would be dispatched to winkle us out of the bars and direct us to weave our bicycles stationwards. The aircraft and the night-flying pupils were waiting to get the show off the ground.

On at least two occasions, I set off into the night sky more than slightly inebriated, with my complement of two navigation pupils and my WOP-AG fearfully, if not soberly, watching my every smallest move. But I got us all down safely and smoothly.

Familiarity bred contempt for, quite convinced that the Anson was an unsinkable machine, some of us unlawfully adopted a casual attitude of dispensing with parachute, mae-west jacket and flying helmet in the interests of personal comfort. I had a set of earphones with microphone attached, and this I would clip over my service-dress cap. But it was not long before an incident let me know the folly of getting airborne without the benefits of safety devices.

One of our pilots was forced down in the Irish Sea with engine failure. Happily, he was wearing his mae-west jacket. But he was also wearing his best uniform — his 'number one blues' — because he wanted to keep an amorous appointment in Blackpool immediately after landing from his flying detail.

He ditched the Anson safely, and the aircraft floated in a convenient manner so that the occupants could launch the inflatable life raft and scramble into the bouncing rubber contraption. Nobby Clark, the pilot, still hoping to keep his tryst on time, and in as immaculate manner as possible, rolled up the legs of his best trousers, removed his shoes and socks and, carrying them in one hand, tried to pick his way through rising water along the wing towards the dinghy. But he fell into the sea up to his neck when he ran out of wing beneath his feet.

The WOP-AG had sent out a mayday signal when disaster became inevitable. A Royal Navy cutter from a nearby warship picked up the four escapees.

Very soon after this incident, the Anson I was flying blew a cylinder in its starboard engine. Fortunately, we were not far from Squires Gate and, as we were on the homeward leg of an exercise, the machine was light in petrol. We were sinking slowly and steadily, because the Anson's one-engine performance was not brilliant. But we made base safely and hit the circuit pattern at about four hundred feet.

About two months after my arrival at Squires Gate I was sent to Edinburgh to appear before a Coastal Command selection board. I passed muster and was appointed to the commissioned rank of acting pilot officer. And, as is the time-honoured custom of the serivce, I was marked for posting to another station. This system, presumably, assists morale by removing the newly-commissioned officer from the coarse badinage of the NCOs, airmen and airwomen with whom he fraternized before he got The Call. I was sent to No 6 Operational Training Unit at Silloth, close to the border of Scotland. I was still a staff pilot and still flying Ansons. But this time I was stooging newly fledged WOP-AGs around the sky.

I was sorry to leave Squires Gate. I got on well with all at the station and my flying abilities were well accepted. Before I left Blackpool I asked my erstwhile flight commander 'Humph' Humphries, by now a squadron leader and Officer Commanding Flying at Squires Gate, how my chances were for returning to the station. He said that he would like me back on the unit and he would see what he could do. His blandishments must have worked. I was at Silloth less than a month.

The work on that northern station was deadly monotonous. I chased drogue-towing aircraft so that my charges could tear off thousands of rounds at the canvas target, and I brooded gloomily over the control column while the pupils bashed off signals and pondered over the morse messages they received.

I was not at Silloth long enough to form any close and lasting associations with any of the fellows there. But the staff NCOs of the flight were a cheerful bunch who, in company with Flight Lieutenant John Bond and myself would, on occasions, travel into Carlisle on our duty-free nights.

A funny little Hornby-type engine would pull the two or three coaches of the train along the few miles of suburban line between Silloth and the city, and Bond and I would sometimes make our way to the engine on the return trip, slip the driver and fireman a couple of bottles of beer, and each try our hands at shovelling coal into the firebox and manipulating the throttle.

I don't know what happened to Bond. He became one of so many faceless, almost forgotten legionaries we met in wartime. I hope he lived through the hostilities. I hope he still lives.

Back at Squires Gate again, I settled well into the easy life. My living quarters were now in the St. Annes Hotel, Lytham, a comfortable bicycle ride from the airfield. Along with a sizeable number of other officers from the station we lived, two to a unit, in the hotel bedrooms with oft-changed sheets on our beds, and with prim and ancient housemaids to tidy up the place. Meals were eaten in the hotel's dining room and we were served by crochety old waitresses, who still clung to the peacetime glories of black uniforms with starched collars, cuffs and frilly white aprons.

We teased them unmercifully as, with poker faces, we would ask for such extravagant dishes as truffles, larks' tongues in honey, and Russian caviar.

'Don't cha' know there's a war on!' they would snap.

In all honesty, I don't think many at Lytham St. Annes or Blackpool did realize that, away down south, bombers were coming over the east coast of England, and RAF men were flying out of their fighter and bomber bases to halt the Luftwaffe and attack German targets. People that Blackpuddlians had never heard of were being killed by hundreds upon hundreds. And our flying jobs at Squires Gate were as safe and as languid as those of peacetime commercial pilots.

'So we've earned a rest,' argued Johnny Johnston, a fellow New

Zealand pilot. Like myself, Johnny had known a bit of a rough time during his first tour of operations. He had been flying Hampdens out of Reykjavik, Iceland, and his last flight in one of those aircraft had ended abruptly when the machine's rudders had locked in a stablized yaw, and Johnny had been obliged to leave the unmanageable beast by means of his parachute.

'Make the most of it,' he counselled. 'The good life won't last forever. We'll both be back on our second tours soon enough.'

But time rolled by and we continued to live easily. Even when we flew a normal quota of trips, our flying times for the month rarely exceeded sixty hours. That was because of the roster system. Johnston and I did in fact want to build up our night air hours, so it was not an uncommon practice for one to accompany the other on a night-flying detail, although not scheduled as a second pilot, so that each of the two- or three-hour trips could be entered in our log-books.

Night flying, until I came to Squires Gate, had amounted to a modest eleven hours and fifty-five minutes in my log-book. And most of that had been flown during my training days. Our work in the Western Desert and Malta had, by its very nature, been almost wholly daytime flying.

I found a fascination in night flying — a feeling that I was sublimely in my true element. I liked the mystery of the darkness, the blue blow-torch flames that came blasting from the exhaust manifolds, the tingling excitement as the aircraft is taxied around the dimly-lit perimeter, the green phosphorescence of the instrument panel, the flarepath suddenly coming alight and stretchng ahead, beckoning. And, as the aircraft rises into the night it becomes your own little principality in the sky — your own little inhabited planet, mingling with a million other stars.

Johnston and I had several calm and uneventful nocturnal excursions together on those flights. A bit of piddling rain was accepted by the officer in charge of night flying as part of the nature of things, and the exercise would proceed with the Ansons splashing their ways along the runway with windscreen wipers swishing and trickles of water oozing in through the cracks in the numerous window frames. In such conditions, with barometric pressures little changed from take-off to touch-down, altimeter readings remained fairly constant. The WAAF girls in flying control, of course, gave incoming pilots the correct reading at base so that the aircrafts' altimeters could be correctly set and, accordingly, the correct height could be assessed.

But Squires Gate lost two aircraft in the Irish mountains while I was at that station. And both crashed at night through dramatic changes in barometric pressure which, in one case, meant that the pilot was actually flying seven hundred feet below the height indicated on his altimeter.

In both instances — well separated by time — the aircraft had taken off in weather that was clear over the west coast of Lancashire. On navigation 'exercises that had them flying north-west towards a landfall near Larne, Northern Ireland, they had run into badly deteriorating weather conditions. Each had flown into a frontal storm of such intensity that the barometric pressure — which governs the functions of an aircraft's altimeter — had led its pilot to believe he had sufficient safety height. Each of those two aircraft had flown into the Antrim Mountains in storm-blinded conditions.

Johnston and I nearly shared such a fate when we were flying together over the same route. We had set off in clear weather. From Squires Gate outward to our first landfall at the Point of Ayre, Isle of Man, the going was fine and the sky was relatively clear and star-powdered. The fine Cheetah-9 engines were purring and the old Aggie Anson was soldiering on at about two thousand feet.

Avro Anson.

Our pupil navigators had given us a reasonable enough course. We had picked up the marine light of the point some miles back and we tracked towards it without having to make much of an adjustment of course to hit it close to ETA. Our pupils, we reckoned, were shaping up competently enough.

I was at the controls when one of the navigators, working feverishly as most of them did, pushed a slip of paper into my hand. It was our next course. I turned up the cockpit light and looked at the figures. I had memorized the mean compass course of all the legs of our regulation navigation exercises, so the information the pupil had handed me was a close enough approximation, drift considered, of the route we should travel towards our next landfall. All was well in our aerial schoolroom.

We found the sky was beginning to cloud and the old Anson was beginning to wallow in the turbulence that had developed. A splatter of rain drummed on the Perspex and I switched on the wipers. We flew onwards, and as our ETA came and passed we peered hopefully for the marine light that was our Northern Ireland landfall. I knew the unexpected strength of the head wind would add a few minutes to the pupils' reckonings. And then, sure enough, the beacon shone through the rain and I asked the navigators for the next course.

After an amount of scuffling and muttering from the navigation table behind me, the slip of paper was forthcoming. Again, I switched on the cockpit light and looked at the new course I had been directed to fly.

I rasped through my microphone, 'What the hell do you think you are doing back there? Do you want to kill all of us?''

'What's the matter, sir?'

'This bloody course — that's the matter. We're supposed to be flying compass course 120 degrees — not your goddamn 220 degrees. That course would take us smack into the Mountains of Mourne, if I accepted your navigation.' I told him other things, too, that his father would have probably denied.

The pupil was terribly sorry. It was a mistake, see! He had written a '2' instead of a '1' on the chit he had handed me. The new course, of course, was one-two-0 — not two-two-0. I was the '2s' duplication — you see!

'Oh, shut up, flight sergeant! Watch it — for Christ's sake watch it!'

So we turn on to a course of 120 degrees. Now we are in pissing rain and it is finding every crack in the Anson's hide. I turn on the landing light. Its beam is muzzled by impenetrable cloud. I check my height. Two thousand feet. We are bucking around in the turbulence so I ease the nose down and drop off height — just a matter of a hundred feet — to try and get out of the overcast. I flick the landing light on and off as I descend lower yet, and the ray bores out into the wider unknown and is shot with bright rods of water that bend and shatter on our windscreen. We are out of cloud. Our height now shows fifteen hundred feet on the altimeter.

Time drags. We rumble on, bucketing and wallowing. I say, needlessly, to Johnston, the two NCO pupil navigators and the staff WOP-AG, 'Keep a watch for the light at Point of Ayre.'

And I flick the switch of the landing light. I gasp, 'Jesus!'

I wrench the handgrips hard to port and kick left rudder frantically. The Anson stands on its red wing-tip light and we pull into a steep turn. Ahead of me is a rugged escarpment of Mount Snaefell, the high peak of the Isle of Man. The frontal system, besides interfering with our altimeter reading, has subjected our aircraft to a hefty drift to starboard.

Soberly we feel our way northways until the flashes of Ayre's marine light are sighted and the point is lying below us. I say to the pupils, quietly: 'Give us a course for base, boys.'

Johnston goes aft. I, too, feel like going to the Elsan.

Now the seat on my starboard side is empty.

Or is it?

I sit in my left-hand seat. Miraculously, it seems, we have come out from under the canopy of cloud. And though the patches of scud I can see the stars and a lunar glow. The control column is in front of me. The throttle pedestal is in the centre of the snug and — now — safe flight deck.

As is my wont, I fly with cockpit lights doused. There are, therefore, no distracting reflections on the windscreen. And so outside signs and events are the more easily discernable. The small battery of dials on the instrument panel glows with green fire, each tiny circle of figures and each trembling little finger a monitor of altitude maintained and velocity achieved, of energy expended and heat controlled. Silently, they report their messages of work steadfastly in progress.

Below us, across the miles that separate our small sky-island from our base, is the Irish Sea, uncluttered by hateful pinnacles of rock. The musical duet from the engines is sweetly synchronized. The storm is behind us.

I have no further cause for doubt or concern. For the Lord is my guardian, my defence at my right hand. The sun will not strike me by day — nor the moon by night.

The author at Burg el Arab, 1942.

A Glenn Martin Baltimore of 69 Squadron, Malta.

Patterns of a night air raid as Malta's ground defences put up an ack-ack barrage.

A Coastal Command Mk V Halifax. These aircraft were used effectively by 502 Squadron, RAF, in convoy escort, anti-submarine and night shipping-strike duties.

The author's Halifax crew at Aldergrove, Northern Ireland, in 1944. Back row: Sgt Ron Morse, F/Sgt Mark Twentyman, Fg Off Roy Rheuben, the author, F/Sgt Stan Sharp. Front: F/Sgt Lloyd Pollard, F/Sgt 'Rum' Rumming, Sgt 'Safe' Keeping, F/Sgt Tom Wellington.

Reunited over a jug of beer in Auckland in 1946: The author (left) with one of his fellow New Zealand crew mates from Malta operations, Wireless-operator air-gunner 'Sonny' Cliffe.

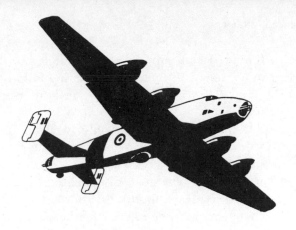

12

Hail to the Halifax

On 6 November 1943 I was married to Dorothy in the Pinner Anglican Church on the outskirts of London. We had become engaged a few months earlier, when I was financially broke — so much so that I had to borrow twenty pounds from the RNZAF Welfare Fund to buy an engagement ring.

The flight lieutenant who held the key to the cashbox at RNZAF Headquarters, London, was a pleasant enough fellow (when he was not pursued by outrageous monetary requests), but he called on God to strike him dead when I told him the reason for my begging. The cash at his disposal, he was careful to point out, was for such common and humanitarian emergencies as getting hung-over airmen back to their distant units after the Piccadilly girls had had their pickings. But I must have touched a chord, for he softened his scolding and gave me a half-smile. Had I any money at home in New Zealand that could be termed collateral? Yes? Good!

'Well,' he said, 'if I advance you this money, will you guarantee to have it refunded?' And he fixed a deadline that could be comfortably met. I said I would and he counted out twenty pound notes. And as I was leaving the office he called after me: 'And don't come back here asking for a loan to buy the wedding ring!'

I had no further cause to seek financial aid from the RNZAF. I became a model of near-abstinence in the officers' messes I was to inhabit henceforth, and I set out upon such a programme of frugality as would have made old Scrooge scratch his pate in puzzlement.

The wedding arrangements and reception, with strong New Zealand representation, were organized by Henry and Molly Loxley Boyle at their home in Pinner. I can happily report that today they are very near and dear to us, they and their family having followed us to New Zealand in the late 1940s. Molly is a New Zealander and her home town is Auckland.

Back at Squires Gate, with a bitter winter well upon us, we pilots and WOP-AGs flew our scheduled exercises through rain, hail and fog. One perishingly cold day, grey with a low overcast, we lost two Ansons and their crews. One just disappeared; and whether the machine and its dead were ever found, I do not know. The other went into the hills somewhere near the town of Clitheroe. How it got there, nobody knows, for dead men cannot speak. Blind in the thick smog, they may have been cruising around looking for a break in the murk. Or they may have been flying a reciprocal heading. Or, ever likely, they could have overshot the airfield on an erroneous ETA.

Several aircraft from Squires Gate flew on searches of the sea and countryside, looking for traces of the missing aircraft but finding nothing. But a few days later a ground party came upon the remains of the Anson that had hit the hill. From the evidence, the crew had been killed instantly.

Soon after Johnny Johnston was posted to a meteorological unit operating out of the Scottish island of Tiree, I was sent to No 1675 Heavy Conversion Unit at Longtown, an airfield close to the border of Scotland. We were both embarking on our second tours. Like Johnston, I would be on Handley Page Halifax four-engined aircraft. I was delighted.

But at Longtown, I found with considerable disappointment that I would have to serve a stint on Coastal Command's Halifax aircraft as a second-pilot. And so I was teamed with a young Canadian pilot of equal rank, Flying Officer Umpherson. He had flown his first operational tour as a second-joe and had thus earned his privilege of qualifying as captain of a Halifax crew.

This was the ruling of Coastal Command. Seemingly, irrespective of a pilot's capabilities, he must first serve in a subordinate role in the starboard seat on the flight deck. So I was to be number two on the totem pole of a nine-man crew — a direction that I'm afraid I took with ill grace. Umpherson was a decent fellow, but several years younger than I. We hit it off well enough and he was appreciative of my grumbles and, I suppose, sympathetic. I suspect he was a little embarrassed having an older man of equal rank and more operational experience his junior in command.

All of the nine members of our crew were strangers to each other, so there was an early shake-down period while we got to know the other fellows' indiosyncrasies. Happily, we were a compatible bunch. Umpherson had flown his first tour on 502 Squadron, which was then based at St. Davids on the outermost promontory of the west coast of Wales. He and his crew, he told us, were to return to that unit as soon as we had gained our proficiency on the conversion course we were now attending.

I reconciled myself to Coastal Command's system. But I was determined to have my own command as soon as I could win the ears and the co-operation of my senior officers. I began by complaining to the officer commanding Longtown. He listened and nodded, and said he understood. He told me to bide my time and state my case to my commanding officer at St. Davids. The course here at Longtown was scheduled to start immediately and he did not want any foul-ups with crew arrangements at this stage.

From the beginning, I found the Halifax a kindly machine. It had, in its large and utilitarian lines, a sort of rugged beauty that endeared it in the eye of the beholder. Not as spirited or as high-flying as her glamorous contemporary, the Avro Lancaster, she was like a plain but golden-hearted girl, whose qualities of the soul showed through, many-splendoured, the longer a man became accustomed to her charms and depended on her graciousness.

As I entered the hatch on the port quarter of E-Easy and followed Umpherson and our instructor, Flight Lieutenant Evans, up the fuselage to the flight deck, I took in the vastness of the aeroplane, compared with the last operational aircraft I had flown. It made the Baltimore's cramped interior seem like the inside of an untidy boilermaker's locker.

I clouted my head on the protrusions from the mid-gunner's turret — something I was fated to do on every subsequent entry up the Halifax fuselage — and passed through the crew rest station to the cockpit.

The machine was dual-controlled, but Evans sat in the captain's left-side seat because this was going to be a familiarization flight. After a short cruise and some accompanying patter from our instructor, Umpherson would occupy the place of honour and take us off and, hopefully, land us safely and soundly. Sergeant Veitch, our flight engineer, took up his post amongst the dials and switches behind the captain's seat. I stood, eyes and ears alert, in the passage space behind the two pilots.

The Halifax Mark II which we were flying was powered by four Rolls-Royce Merlin engines. They were fed, through an intricate system of leads and petrol cocks, by a battery of twelve fuel tanks capable of holding a total capacity of almost nineteen hundred gallons of high-octane petrol. On the instrument panel in front of the two pilots were something like forty dials, buttons and levers. In the flight engineer's compartment were forty-four assorted gauges, knobs and tits. Veitch, watching his engine temperatures, oil pressures and fuel levels, would be a busy lad.

Instructor Evans began to run through the list of vital procedures necessary to bring the huge sleeping aircraft to life. And Umpherson made his responses, nodding his head and murmuring his understandings of each move. Quietly and probably a little impatiently, he listened. He had learned his cockpit drill over many hours and many air miles of take-offs, landings, coastwise patrols and sea searches — all leading up in readiness for this occasion.

Veitch, his head full of early ground-training school theory, peered around the side of the bulkhead that divided him from the cockpit. He and I, lesser players in this performance, listened to the litany and hoped to benefit from the words of experience and sagacity that poured from the mouth of Evans.

The sergeant's expectations of higher glories in wartime were slim. In time, a flight sergeant's brass crowns might surmount his chevrons. And, if he was good at his trade, fortunate in dodging death and provided the war lasted long enough, he might rise in rank to become a warrant officer. He would get a bit more in his pay packet, and officers, if they remembered custom and should the fancy so move them, would call him 'Mister'. If a lot of his contemporaries were killed off, so lessening the challenges of competition, he could by great fortune make commissioned rank. Who knows — he might even become a station engineer officer, secure in his ground job and proud of his squadron leader status?

Me? I wanted captaincy of a Halifax. I wanted to sit in the left seat of one of those magnificent monsters and, with my own skills and firm hands, lift sixty thousand pounds of laden aircraft off the runway and guide it into the haunted night. I wanted, so earnestly, the power and the glory of that role.

I watched every move attentively. I listened so very carefully.

One by one, beginning with the port outer engine, the Rolls-Royce Merlins coughed into life with a cloud of grey smoke. They ran quietly as the oil warmed and circulated through their veins and their lungs, like blood moves in a human's limbering muscles and organs.

Evans switched on the DR compass and set about checking temperatures and pressures, the functioning of flaps, the Pesco pumps and the inter-communication system. He ran the number one engine to fifteen hundred revolutions and tested each of its two magnetos. Then he pushed the throttle lever steadily forward while he pulled the control column hard back and anchored it to his stomach with his left arm. The engine rumbled a plus-four boost while he checked the two-speed supercharger and the functioning of the constant-speed propeller.

There was a thundering and an exciting vibration throughout the aircraft as Evans moved the throttle to take-off power and took notice of the boost reading. When he pulled back the power to plus-nine boost, he checked again for magneto drop. He went through the same ritual with each of the other three engines, fighting the kicking control column as the turbulence buffeted against the aircraft's elevators and rudders. And when he was satisfied that every dial showed its norm or therm, power or pressure, he waved to the ground crew to drag away the chocks from the wheels and he gunned the big aircraft forward.

Evans used a minimum of brake pressure as he taxied around the perimeter path towards the take-off end of the runway, relying expertly on his inboard engines to swing the Halifax around the curves of the asphalt track. He stopped the aeroplane across-wind before he came to the runway threshold, and commanded Umpherson's attention to the vital take-off procedures as he began his check drill.

'Auto controls; main switch off — clutch in — gyro out — and move the controls to ensure they're free.' He went through the full travels of simulated dive and climb, left and right bank. They were free. 'Trimming tabs; rudder and aileron controls neutral — elevator half a division tail-heavy.' Evans' eyes and his right hand explored the trim wheels and the datum marks. 'Propellers; speed controls up for increased revs. Fuel; check that cocks are set okay. Sergeant Veitch — are all three cross-fed cocks off for take-off. Are tanks one and three open?

Veitch acknowledges.

'Flaps,' continues Evans. 'We select thirty-five degrees for take-off.' He pushes the lever and watches the indicator gauge alongside the

DR compass until the needle shows at almost three o'clock on the dial. 'That'll get us airborne quickly on this shortish runway.'

There is yet more to come. A big aircraft — a big checklist. And there would be a correspondingly big crash if any vital part of the cockpit drill should be overlooked.

'Superchargers; M ratio — radiators shut — air intake, cold. Boost control cut-out; correct position — throttle gate open.'

The master is now getting near the end of his performance. He looks at Umpherson; and then he half turns and addresses Veitch and me. 'Crew at stations?' We tell him, yes. 'Hatches closed?' Again, we acknowledge.

Evans calls the control tower, and concurrent with the WAAF's lilting soprano voice that gives us permission to take off we get the beam of green from the Aldis lamp. Our pilot moves the Halifax forward and turns it into wind with the brakes groaning. He lets the machine run forward a yard or two to set the tail wheel straight and aims its nose along the centre of the runway. His right hand moves the four throttle levers forward slowly, the port engines getting a little more power than those on the right, because of the aircraft's tendency to swing on its torque to the left. Umpherson's left hand is right behind the captain's throttle grip, ready to hold and clamp the levers firm in full-power position as soon as Evans has pushed them full travel to the gate.

Umpherson chants assurances as Evans, with his two hands now on the control grips, and concentrates on ruddering a straight course along the runway, waiting for the moment when he can lift the aeroplane into the air. 'Revs okay — boost okay — speed okay — temperatures okay!' These are the words the captain likes to hear. He has a lot of aircraft on his hands at this time.

Evans feels, by the seat of his pants, that it is time to become airborne. At just under ninety knots the Halifax is ready and the pilot eases back on the control column and we leave the ground, roaring upwards, an island in the air.

Up come the wheels, nestling into their bays with dull thumps. And up comes the thirty-five degrees of flap. And we are soon flying high. Evans, demonstrating the aircraft's ability to fly with diminished power, feathers the port-outer propeller and cuts the engine. The three-bladed airscrew fluffs lazily around and then becomes still and strangely stark. He adjusts the trim and the Halifax trundles along, its number two engine doing a bit more work to compensate for its sleeping partner on the port wing.

Evans looks around his audience of three and pulls power off the energetic port-inner motor. He grins as he feathers that propeller, also. The big white aeroplane is shouldering and soldiering along, kept aloft only by the two starboard power plants.

Evans says: 'She'll gradually sink, because she's a fairly old crate and has lost a lot of her guts. But in a pinch, the Halifax will get you closer to home that you'd realize, on just two motors.'

He cruises the machine along for a minute or two in this lame state before he sets the port propellers windmilling and gives the engines back their life. He climbs higher, throttles back all the motors and eases back slightly on the control column. The airspeed drops away to ninety-five knots and the Halifax drops her nose in a gentle, straight stall. No hysterical judderings. No vicious flipping of a wing or petulant dive. It is a very kindly, civilized aeroplane.

Evans shows us steep turns and demonstrates the approved evasive action we should adopt if pursued by enemy fighters — a manoeuvre called the 'Lancaster corkscrew'. And then he returns us to Longtown, rumbling in on the landing approach at one hundred knots. We come over the threshold and he holds the big machine level. The tyres brush the runway with little yelps of protest and we are running along the strip at eighty knots. We are slowed by gentle braking and the Halifax is turned off the runway. It is now Umpherson's turn to sit in the left seat and take us aloft.

Umpherson did not take long to get off solo in the Halifax. He was a steady, methodical pilot and I felt quite safe in his keeping. Sergeant Veitch and I accompanied our new master on his circuits-and-landings exercises, and a couple of days later our full crew of nine piled into Halifax A-Able and went on a local shake-down jaunt over northern England and some of the border country of Scotland. We flew over Gretna Green, the fabled wedding goal of runaway lovers, which is not far from Longtown. And we winged onward past Ecclefechan, where that craggy genius Carlyle was born, to Dumfries. Here it was that ploughman-poet Robert Burns spent his last tragic days. And from there we turned to starboard and flew inland, away from the shores of Solway Firth and over the rising land of Roxburghshire to the headwaters of the River Teviot.

As a native of sparsely populated New Zealand, it had long been my belief before I visited Britain that this kingdom's milling millions must be spread thickly over most of the British Isles. Not so. For in our Halifax we flew onwards for mile upon mile and saw nothing below us but bleak and forbidding heather country, with no sign of life but the occasional white specks that were sheep.

Years ago, through the misty glens rode fierce moss-troopers on their shaggy horses, moving down to the border under the light of the moon to harry the English and drive off their cattle. Under us lay Hawick. And soon, showing through the haze, appeared the gaunt skeleton of Jedburgh's ruined abbey. Close by the venerable masonry was the old house where Mary Queen of Scots lay desperately ill after her wild ride to visit her wounded lover, Bothwell, at Hermitage Castle.

We moved in aerial company with ghosts.

Our training continued. Umpherson was checked out on his night-flying circuits and we later flew on air-to-air gunnery exercises, photographic, low-level bombing and fighter-affiliation manoeuvres. Our crew was settling down well, each man getting used to his fellows' mannerisms and flight procedures. And we had a practical demonstration, too, of how our young captain could respond in a grave emergency.

We had been briefed to fly a navigation exercise that was to take us along the Solway Firth, by way of Silloth, to the Point of Ayre on the Isle of Man. From there we were to make for the coast of Northern Ireland before returning home.

After we had become airborne I was sitting back in my starboard seat, listening to the beat of the four engines and looking through the arc of the starboard-inner propeller to the faint mist that was the speeding number four airscrew. This was our means of assessing fine adjustment of engine synchronization. After we had taken the voom-voom-voom out of the four motors' roaring, we looked through the fast-revolving propeller blades. If there was a slow-moving shadow like an airscrew blade coursing backwards within the arcs, a slight throttle correction was still needed.

But what I did see sent a chill down my backbone and made the chemicals rush into my bloodstream. The starboard-inner engine, without warning, threw out a great blossom of flame.

'Fire!' I yelled. 'Starboard-inner on fire!'

Umpherson seemd to do his three vital moves all at once. He pulled back the throttle of the sick motor, reached for the fire-extinguisher box and stabbed the number three button, and reached to the roof panel and feathered the propeller.

For a few twittery moments it seemed that the flames would grow. A long stream of fire was trailing aft across the top of the wing. We were at only one thousand feet, which was too low for the safe use of parachutes, should the blazing engine spread its mischief. So, if the fire should gain, our chances of a safe landing were slim.

But the extinguisher had injected its goo into the engine's system and had done a good job. The fiery banners died in black smoke, and Umpherson and I looked at each other and shook our heads, silently and eloquently. We called the control tower, got our landing clearance and came in with our number three propeller standing still and gaunt, and our engine cowling scorched.

So, I thought, out of a clear sky comes a cloud of evil no bigger than a man's hand. Umpherson's cockpit drill had not flushed from cover the demons that had been lurking in the engine's intricate system of wires and pipelines. Nor had the full-powered thundering of the aircraft along the runway shown up an malfunctioning on take-off. In fact, when the stress was off the engines, the temperamental number three motor decided to quit. So who could tell when disaster might come?

Umpherson and Veitch and I tried to discover the reason for the fire. But all we got were shrugs and apologetic grins from the engineer officer and his NCOs. It was just one of those things.

'Gremlins,' laughed one of the aircraftman fitters.

13
Second Tour

When we had proved our proficiency as a Halifax crew ready for operational flying, we were posted to 502 Squadron, then stationed at St. Davids in Wales. This was Umpherson's old unit and he was back with his companions again. We, this new-found crew, slipped quietly into the routine of this Coastal Command squadron that was, at that time, engaged in anti-submarine work in the Bay of Biscay and the occasional convoy-guard stint in Western Approaches.

After my months of stooging around the Irish Sea, I was now keen to get into more active flying again. My nerves were no longer twanging like piano wires, my pelvis was not aching and, although I still wore a lean and hungry look, I was sleeping well and feeling fit. But I wanted my own command of a Halifax and I knew the only way to gain that status was to gather experience on operational sorties.

Umpherson was still required to fly his training exercises involving radar, bombing, BABS landings and flare-dropping flights. Naturally, as one of his crew, I was involved in those manoeuvres. But when I heard that Flight Lieutenant Pruden's second pilot was ill, I volunteered for the vacant slot and went off on an anti-submarine box patrol off the coast of Brest.

Pruden, I discovered with sympathy and some concern for our mutual well-being, was in need of a rest from flying. He showed all the signs of a pilot who had logged too many hours of operational flying. On our first take-off run he let the characteristic torque of the Halifax take over and the aircraft bored off to the left beyond the bounds of safety. Pruden had to haul back the throttle levers and stamp on the brakes as the machine left the runway and blazed trails in the rough grass. He trundled the aeroplane back to the end of the runway and tried again. And after a nerve-twanging yaw to port, the great beast left the ground with one wheel bouncing along on the turf.

For the next few days I gave my services to both Umpherson and Pruden in matters of both patrols and practice bombing, radar, gunnery, navigation and flare-dropping exercises. We were involved in lots of practice flying on the squadron as, besides our operational work in attacking enemy submarines and surface shipping in the illumination from chandelier flares, we were developing the techniques of detecting the movements of submerged submarines by the use of sonic buoys. Royal Navy submarines were co-operating in some of those exercises, and by and large there was a spirit of great camaraderie between the two services. But there was one occasion when some of the wooden battens we were using as dummy bombs hit the conning tower of a surfaced vessel and dented the plates. The submarine's commander was so cross about the affair that he took his tin boat home and wouldn't play anymore.

When Pruden's second pilot was well enough to join his crew mates again, I opted to fill another temporary vacancy and flew as Squadron Leader Hannah's mate in the cockpit. Hannah was an Australian with a fiercely efficient manner and a bottom jaw that jutted out belligerently. Unlike most of his countrymen, he did not smile easily. Nor did he storm around, shouting out rude and noisy adjectives or earthy expletives. Probably he had been a Sydney banker or stockbroker in earlier and more peaceful times. I do not believe he had ever heard of the Black Stump, much less the wild coarse outback land that lay beyond that demarcation line. He was the antithesis of your popular 'dinkum Aussie'. He had dark hair, brushed straight back from his forehead and gummed in place by an oleaginous, perfumed dressing. And this, along with his gimlet gaze, his square jaw and his suave black hairline moustache, reminded us of a notable character in the American comic strips of the day. We called him Fearless Fosdick.

On our first trip together we went on a patrol off the French coast, bay-crawling down to Lorient by the dawn's early light and scuttling at wave-top level when the inevitable enemy fighters appeared. For almost twelve hours we co-operated with the Navy in covering an area of hostile coastline where a Liberator bomber of Coastal Command had earlier attacked a U-boat. But, as our petrol ran low, we had to leave the scene to the scrutiny of the sailors and return to St. Davids.

After several more exercise flights with my official skipper, I went on my first operational sortie with Umpherson. This was more than a month after we had arrived at St. Davids from Longtown. As was the case with my trips with Pruden and Hannah, the brief called for a patrol off Brest, Lorient and St. Nazaire. We set off at night and spent six and a half hours in darkness, prowling off-shore with our WOP-AGs taking their half-hour watches on the radar scanner. We hung around until dawn revealed the coast of France grey, forbidding and very close. But we had no sightings on the radar screen and we left the scene in a hurry when two Ju-88s showed against the lightening sky.

Dorothy visited me while I was at St. Davids. When we found that she could get a few days' leave, I went into the village (which is, of course, a cathedral city) and rented a bedroom from a Mrs Davis. She was suspicious of airmen generally and, I believe, of me in particular. I had 'New Zealand' emblazoned on my shoulder flashes, and to this stolid Welshwoman I could be either a ruffian All Black rugby player or a savage. Or probably both. And whereas she did not ask to see tangible evidence of my marriage to an English girl, she was clearly standing no hanky-panky. But I continued to talk convincingly and, on a subsequent visit to try and clinch the deal, I brought with me a few photographs of the wedding at Pinner-in-the-Vale. Mrs Davis was at once happy and co-operative.

Dorothy arrived by rail after several changes of trains. We spent a weekend together in the quaint little township, wandering the cliffed coastline and strolling through the ancient cathedral of St. Davids.

From without, the venerable old building gives the impression of austerity. But within, its decorated nave and high fretted arches, its beautiful rood-screen, its bishop's throne and its choir stalls convey past splendours still majestic, and devotion everlasting. We stepped reverently beneath its time ravaged timbers and touched the powdering masonry. We peered through the chinks of the aeons-old tombs and saw the dusty bones of high clerics and proud noblemen long gone from Wales and this earthly world. We marvelled at the travel of the years.

Immediately after Dorothy's return to London, I had news from Wing Commander Maton, the commanding officer of our squadron at St. Davids, that my constant bitching and bellyaching for my own command had paid off. I had been pestering him, his adjutant and his flight commanders for a captaincy rating ever since I arrived on the station. And so, after a month and five days of being with the squadron, I was being posted back to No 1674 Heavy Conversion Unit, which by this time had moved its headquarters to Aldergrove in County Antrim, Northern Ireland.

Wing Commander Maton, who wore the brevet of a WOP-AG, grinned as he bade me farewell in his office. He said he had been impressed with my enthusiasm and he would be very happy to have me back on the squadron strength with my new crew. I went on my way, walking on air.

Aldergrove, I found, was a long-established RAF station close to the shores of Lough Neagh and not many miles from Belfast. It was, in fact, the home base of 502 Squadron, which was an Auxiliary 'county' squadron adopted by Ulster. The unit's badge incorporated the traditional Red Hand motif of Northern Ireland.

After the Irish Sea ferry landed me at Belfast, I travelled by RAF motor transport to the airfield and checked in at the administration office. I soon discovered that I had inherited eight-ninths of an original Liberator crew which had done its training in the Bahamas. The captain of the team, the ninth man, had been posted to another squadron while his eight companions had been transferred to Aldergrove, hopefully to serve under the command of the second pilot, Warrant Officer Mark Twentyman, who had been expecting to qualify for his captaincy.

This was not to be. Mark Twentyman and his band found themselves, after the sophistication of the Yankee Liberator bombers, relegated to (their) rather despised Halifax buses. And that was not all. They were to be subservient to an outsider as their skipper. In a word — me.

But we soon settled down. I sympathized with Twentyman, for I knew he felt exactly the same as I had done when I had to become Umpherson's second-joe. He took his disappointment reasonably well and I soon found he was a damn fine fellow to have alongside me on the flight deck.

Twentyman was a man in his mid-twenties, with red hair and a freckled complexion. He was a steady, unflappable soul with a nice sense of dry humour. His home town was, I believe, Sheffield.

My new-found navigator was Roy Rheuben, an Australian by birth, American by adoption and a serving officer in the Royal Canadian Air Force with the rank of flying officer. The circumstances of that United Nations mix resulted from his moving to Los Angeles with his parents. But before he could take out United States naturalization papers, war had broken out. So, still being a British subject — and a very loyal one — he crossed the border into Canada and joined the country's Air Force.

The senior WOP-AG of the team was Flight Sergeant Rumming, an Englishman who usually took over the working of the radar when a sighting was picked up on the instrument's scanner. His three companions who worked on a roster system at the radar screen, and who shuttled positions between the gun turrets and stints on the wireless set, were Australian sergeants.

Stan Sharp came from Newcastle in New South Wales. He was in his early twenties. Lloyd Pollard and Tom Wellington were both boys of nineteen. Lloyd was a young bank clerk with the Commercial Bank of Sydney. Tom, who never had any name but Wimpy, had a post office job in Ayr, Northern Queensland, before the war.

Our flight engineer was another nineteen-year-old. Ron Morse's home was at Walton-on-Thames. And our ninth man, Keeping, was a straight air gunner. Inevitably, he was called 'Safe'. I never did find out what his baptismal name was.

A couple of days after I had met my crew, Mark Twentyman, Ron Morse and I were taken aloft in Halifax E-Easy, under the control of Flight Lieutenant Hunter, and after two-and-a-half hours of dual circuits and landings, I was flying solo and liking the experience very much. Flight Lieutenant Taffy Evans, the same officer who had sent Umpherson off solo a few weeks earlier, was now my instructor and we hit it off easily.

We practised three-engined overshoots, which meant trundling the aeroplane in with one propeller feathered and giving the three live motors the gun to climb away from the field again, simulating a mis-landing. We flew photographic exercises; and we tried our techniques on the Mark 3 bombsight, using dummy missiles. Later in the course we practised with the more sophisticated Mark 14 bombsight and exercised frequently on radar manoeuvres.

We had a memorable night-flying navigation exercise that took us out into the reaches of the Atlantic in our radar search for the pin-prick pinnacle of Rockall, a small pyramid of rock, covered with white bird dung, that sticks up out of the grey ocean miles away from the west coast of Ireland. We had to proceed by dead recokoning, find the target on our radar screen, and return to base from that small landfall. Normally, the exercise should have been a piece of cake. But we ran into a shocking storm and, to add to our discomfort, the starboard-inner engine gave trouble. We had to feather the propeller and come bouncing and wallowing through the gale on three engines to make a dawn touch-down at Aldergrove.

I can say, without hesitation, that those hours of that night exercise were the most turbulent I have ever known in an aircraft. The poor old Halifax went up and down like a crazy elevator, but at no stage did I ever doubt the machine's sturdiness or its ability to get us home on her three motors. I had liked the Halifax from the first moment I flew as a passenger with Evans and Umpherson at Longtown. After that trip to Rockall I was wholly dedicated to the aeroplane.

While we were still at Aldergrove, I heard that Umpherson and his crew had stood into danger while on a reconnaissance off the French coast. He had taken his Halifax in close to Lorient and had been jumped by enemy fighters. Flight Sergeant Davies, his senior WOP-AG, had been hit by a fragment of cannon shell. He had survived the long haul homewards in the damaged aircraft but died soon after he was admitted to the sick quarters at St. Davids. Umpherson and the rest of the crew escaped serious injury.

We enjoyed our stay in Northern Ireland. The Ulster people, far happier in those days than they are now, were wonderfully hospitable. Roy Rheuben and I were invited to spend a weekend in a grand old mansion close to Portrush. Our host, an elderly squire whose ancestors had owned the property for centuries, took us around the district and showed us the fascinating Giants Causeway. We got to know Belfast well, too, and all of us were reluctant to leave Aldergrove when our course ended.

We acquitted ourselves well in our Halifax conversion exercises, and our assessment as an operationally-ready crew was 'above average' when we were posted to 502 Squadron.

Time and tide, and the strategies of war, wait for no man. I found that our squadron had moved from St. Davids and was now stationed at Stornoway, on the east coast of the island of Lewis, in the Outer Hebrides. We had our day or two of leave after our training days at Aldergrove and I went home to London — home being a small flat that Dorothy had managed to rent in Pinner. And then I proceeded by rail to Inverness, where I boarded a small train that took me to the ferry and the boat trip across the North Minch.

Stornoway was not as cold as we had expected, despite the fact that we arrived in this northerly spot in the darkening days of early winter.

An explanation that we had heard advanced was that the warm waters of the North Atlantic Drift, an extension of the Gulf Stream, flowed upwards past the Outer Hebrides and so kept the worst of the snow away. But we did get fog, and we certainly did have glazed ice on the runways at some most inconvenient times, despite the alleged balm of the far-wandering warm current. We slept in Nissen huts, those corrugated iron shelters like half-round sections of gigantic water tanks. Fortunately, they had wooden floors. What they were like in summer I do not know; but sleeping under their cover in winter was only made bearable by the continual stoking of the iron stove which was standard equipment in each hut. The uninsulated iron shells caught and held the chilled air borne on the perishing wind and fought against the therms that we tried bake out of the fast-emptying coal boxes.

Along with 502 Squadron at Stornoway was another Halifax unit, 58 Squadron, which was engaged in the same type of work as our

A Halifax of 203 Squadron attacking a German submarine.

aircraft and crews. Since our unit had moved from St. Davids it had been given the role of an anti-shipping strike force, and our search and attack territory was now mainly the Narrow Seas — the Skagerrak and Kattegat — bounded by the shores of Norway, Sweden and Denmark.

Enemy ships were bringing supplies down from German-occupied Oslo, Kristiansand and Stavanger. They would move south, passing between Skagen and Göteborg on their way to Kiel. There was also a considerable amount of enemy waterborne traffic moving northwards.

Our aircraft, each with a load of six 500-pound bombs, and a number of chandelier flares, would set off by night to find such targets by radar sightings. The area was hazardous. As the waterways were tightly surrounded by both hostile and neutral lands, it was inevitable that every movement of our aircraft was tracked by enemy electronic recorders. So bright-eyed and aggressive German night-fighter pilots would be directed on to our machines, and it was not surprising that our ship-hunting squadrons lost several crews within the first few weeks of those operations.

Poor old Pruden, with whom I had flown on my first operational sortie after joining 502 Squadron, did not bring his crew home after just such a mission around the Kattegat.

Our first flying exercise after we arrived at Stornoway was a practice bombing run using the Mark 3 bombsight. We had about an hour-and-a-half of daylight bombing before we went aloft again that night, loaded with practice missiles and chandelier flares. The technique was to home in on the marine target by the aid of radar, drop our flares to illuminate the quarry, make a fast turn and then run in for the bomb-drop.

We practised this method (using illuminating flares only, of course) by stalking co-operative Navy MTBs in local waters. I have no idea how the *matelots* reacted to being so suddenly displayed, like clandestine lovers when a car's headlight picks them out in a roadside meadow. But the technique was quite literally illuminating. The method had its disadvantages, too. By throwing a spotlight on the quarry we were also making known our presence. In the case of the enemy, the target ship and her escorts would throw up a lot of flak at the bright white undersides of our wings and fuselage, and the diligent German night-fighters could gravitate towards the scene of much candlepower with high hopes of a kill.

That was the system of night bombing used by the two squadrons when we first began searching the narrow seas of Scandinavia. We patrolled throughout the whole of the sortie at the minimum safe bombing height of twelve hundred feet. We were using bombs with air-burst pistols, which meant that as the missiles approached the surface of the sea, the forward pressure of air built up against the density of the water was sufficient to trigger the sensitive mechanism of the nose fuses and cause the bombs to explode, with frightful fragmentation, on the wave tops. A stick of six 500-pounders, spaced about 120 feet apart, could cause much havoc, alarm and despondency as it straddled the target. Captured seamen from such stricken ships gave testimony to the dread they all had of these weapons.

A cruising height of twelve hundred feet was an open invitation for enemy interceptor aircraft to be directed against us. German tracking stations were strategically placed, and we were continually on their electronic screens from before we entered the Skagerrak until we were on the way home — if, indeed, we managed to elude the night-fighters. But the cunning and skills of the British boffins and missiles experts were devising new methods of attack and it did not take long before a system of ship bombing by the aid of radar was evolved. This did away with the need to turn Scandinavian waters into a torchlight tattoo arena. The move to dispense with chandelier flares was greeted with much rejoicing in the crew rooms.

This left the aircrews with only two main remaining concerns about the sorties: the fact that our aircraft, now working solely at night, were still painted in Coastal Command's daytime livery of all-white; and the fact that we still had to trundle all the way around the patrol area at twelve hundred feet.

With regard to the first complaint, camouflage experts from Group Headquarters tried to explain their theories of refractive indices, and sought to convince us that white aircraft were as invisible as black machines in the dark — a theory that was not accepted by the fellows who had to fly the pallid machines. But it was significant that, soon after the debate, our Halifax fleet soon became sombre, matt-black monsters.

On the matter of our operational height when flying our sorties, the belief was held, by bombing experts, that we would not be able to pick up a satisfactory radar sighting from any worthwhile distance if we flew too low. Our machines were equipped with radio altimeters, clever devices which bounced electronic signals off the ground or the surface of the sea and measured the distance by impulses. Some of the pilots therefore began to experiment by flying low, aided by the radio altimeters.

They discovered that at a cruising height of only two hundred feet they could capture a pretty clear radar sighting at a distance of twelve miles and home their aircraft on to the 'blip' without any trouble. As they ran up on the target they would begin to climb to the safe bombing height of twelve hundred feet. Then the pilot, the navigator-bomb aimer and the radar operator, working as a precision team, would make the bombing run, drop the load, and then scuttle down to the comparative safety of two hundred feet again.

The reason for such low flying was to lessen the chances of the aircraft being picked up by the enemy's electronic scanners and to deny hostile night-fighters the opportunity of either flying under our belly or committing themselves to headlong dives at us.

Patrols at two hundred feet soon became the order of the day or, more precisely, the night. The radio altimeter had a tolerance of ten feet either side of the flying height selected and set on the instrument.

A Halifax shipping strike in the Kattegat.

Three lights on its panel, not unlike the common traffic-lights system, gave clear warnings and assurances of actual cruising heights. If the glow showed green the pilot knew that he was flying within the twenty-foot tolerance of the height he had selected. If it was red he knew (for a short time, at least) that he was too low. An amber light indicated that the aircraft was flying too high.

We did a lot of practice flying, and as we were now in a unit that operated mainly under the cover of darkness, many of our exercises involved night flying. We brushed up on our studies of astro-navigation and diligently filled in our Form 1599 sight log-books. With the Mark 9A sextant we shot the sun by day, and the moon and Altair and Dhube, Polaris and Arcturus by night. We took our instructions from our navigation and armaments tutors, and we collected our data from the intelligence and meteorological officers. We climbed into our duralumin capsule and switched on dim yellow lights. We wove our spells and chanted our incantations, murmuring our parts in the ceremony and pressing vital buttons that gave us power and privilege. And when we were satisfied with our earthly magic, we moved with much noise and took our mischief into the dark sky.

And so we travelled our errands between Sagittarius and Sirius, Formalhaut and Spica, moving with purpose and direction through the night.

14

A Night over Narrow Seas

The night is wet — which is not unusual at Stornoway in the winter. The nine of us in our Halifax crew have sat through sortie briefings and have heard the words of wisdom and counsel from our intelligence, navigation, gunnery, armament and wireless officers; and we have heeded the sounds of warning from the meteorological soothsayer. The gloomy frontal system could, and should, pass through before long; and this being the case, we would be flying in fairly clear air after the rain did its dash. But we were to keep out of cloud. The icing level was well down. 'So keep low, chaps. Keep low!'

Low? How low does one fly around the Norwegian fjords? How nonchalant can one get about low-flying height over places like Kristiansund, Alesund and Nordfjordeld, where all the snowy hills run steeply down to the twisty maze of inlets? The drooping clouds over Romsdale, Sogn and Fjordane would have hard centres. And below these canopies of mist would be the vigilant gun-crews of the enemy — shore-based anti-aircraft men and shipboard cannoneers, shivering at their breeches and in their britches.

We have been told our mission. We are to search for ships. We are to keep a radar watch along the western coast of Norway; and we are to drop flares in several fjords within our search area, hopefully that we may sight and bomb the vessels.

Since the liberation of France, Coastal Command has had new problems. Before the Overlord invasion, Brest, St Nazaire, Lorient, La Pallice and Bordeaux were Germany's key U-boat stations. But with the neutralization of those ports, Norwegian harbours have assumed a new importance. They have, of course, been used a good deal by the enemy since the occupation of Norway. Now they are the only bases from which German submarines can venture to maraud in the Atlantic.

So, in September 1944, Coastal Command intensifies its anti-U-boat patrols in northern waters and steps up operations against enemy shipping plying between the German Baltic ports and Danish and Norwegian harbours. When the Germans used the French ports, U-boats could be supplied by land communications across occupied Europe. It was not easy for the Allies to stop the traffic. But the Norwegian bases have to be supplied mainly by sea. And the Scandinavian waters have become a gauntlet-run for the enemy.

For the Germans, a difficult situation has been created by the defection of Finland; and this has been further aggravated by Sweden's refusal to allow German troops on her railways. Germany's problem is therefore a dual one. First, she must ensure that her U-boats get oil, torpedoes and the mass of other requirements needed for ocean patrols; and secondly, she has to keep open her lines of communication with her troops in northern Norway, where her position is becoming steadily more precarious.

Since evacuation of the extreme north of Norway and of Finland enables a number of divisions to be detailed for more urgent duties on the Western and Eastern fronts, there is now no doubt that substantial transfers of troops are taking place. Thus, the sea routes along the coast of Norway and across the Skagerrak and Kattegat have become the main arteries of supply and troop-carrying traffic. And the enemy gives this shipping all the protective cover it can afford.

So our harassments are not treated with disdain.

We have two enemy camps through which we must travel tonight. One is man-made, and its policy is that attack is the best means of defence. The other, and perhaps the more ominous foe, is the weather.

We have collected our coffee and sandwiches from the duty cooks and the kitchen WAAFs. And the shivering MT driver picks us up outside the operations room and we pile into the canopied half-tonner.

She is a plain blonde, not long emerged from childhood. 'Which is your kite, luv?' she asks.

'Around by "A" Flight', I tell her. I point into the gloom. 'Keep going that way — around the perimeter. I'll say when to stop.'

'Christ, you've got a hell of a night for it, 'aint you.' She crouches over the wheel, bundled in her greatcoat and her voice comes muffled through the weave of her scarf. She peers through the streaming windscreen at the asphalt track that is faintly lit by the cowled headlights.

'It gets better, the further we fly — so we've been led to believe.'

'Long trip, luv?'

'Ten — eleven hours, maybe. Might be more.'

'Jesus. Rather it wus you than me!'

I see the thin shafts of torch beams interlaced with rods of rain. I tell the girl: 'There, that's the one.'

She slows the half-tonner and turns it off the perimeter track, easing it carefully towards the Halifax that looms big and sombre in the filtered headlight glow.

We tumble out of the MT vehicle, dragging parachute bags and navigation kit; food packs; flying helmets that trail flexes and microphone mouth-pieces and bayonet plugs; mae-west life jackets; and radar and wireless log-books. We clump hurriedly to the wide shelter of the aircraft's port wing, where the ground crew of B-Baker are holding conference.

The WAAF driver, happier and more unbending in her own social climate among the fitters and riggers, makes a few passes of robust repartee before she gets back into the cab of her vehicle.

Then she discovers my food pack still lying on the seat beside her. She calls: ''Ere, Skipper — you've nearly gorn wivout your bloomin' supper!'

I tell her: 'Thanks, girl.' Was any knight at the lists ever offered a more practical favour before the joust?

Knights? We stamp around in our modern armour, laughing and mildly oathing, with just a little too much nervous banter. Our breastplates are leather Irvin jackets which, like our calf-high boots, are wool-lined. Our helmets are soft and pliable, and our emergency flying goggles are the visors. Our gauntlets are grey and greasy silk gloves that once were white. Technically, they should be worn beneath our cumbersome leather gauntlets; but we prefer the freedom of touch allowed by skin-snugging, warmth-sealing silk as we flick switches, turn knobs and twist dials.

We talk with the ground crew's flight sergeant, who tells us that all is well with our machine. Mark Twentyman and I have been this way, earlier in the evening; before darkness set in we wandered around the Halifax, looking at all the engine panels for traces of oil leaks, checking against sprung rivets, examining every foot of the main-plane's leading edge, ensuring that cowlings were snug, studying the huge tyres for cuts in the surfaces and noting that there was no creep of the cases beyond the safety marks painted on the wheel rims.

We ran our critical eyes over the oleo legs and the brake-fluid pressure lines of the undercarriage; and we moved aft to inspect the anti-freeze grease that covered the hinges of the rudders and the elevators. We checked the static head of the pressure anemometer and the movements of the turrets. We saw that the aircraft's safety equipment was in order. The medical kits — aye, and the Elsan toilet, too — passed our daylight scrutiny.

Now that darkness was upon us, we made our final external inspections of the vital parts of the machine. We double-checked that the pitot-head cover was removed so that we would not be denied an airspeed reading. And by torchlight we ran our hands over the elevators and diligently searched the tail structure, ensuring that the external locking clamps had been removed by the riggers. We moved forward again and shone our torches on the tyres and upwards against the under-bellies of the engine pods. We kicked the wedge-shaped wheel chocks, satisfying ourselves that they were snugly in place.

Niggling? Not when nine lives are in my care. Not when just one fiddling little oversight could foul up this great sixty-thousand-pound-weight of bombed-up Halifax. Care — meticulous care — is the watchword.

The others of our crew are, by now, within the aircraft. Twentyman and I clamber up through the hatch in the port quarter and make our way along the sloping aisle towards the flight deck. Inevitably, I clout my head against the nether knobs of the dorsal turret's mechanism as I move through the dim innards of B-Baker. And I curse loudly, which is, of course, also inevitable.

There is a corporal fitter sitting on my throne in the cockpit. Earlier, he has had the engines running and checked them for boost output and constancy of revolutions. He and his flight-sergeant are happy enough with their team's ministrations, he tells me. So I leave him to his final adjustments while I move around inside the aircraft, making a final inspection, noting that all loose equipment has been stowed and that the turrets are set at control and centred. I look at switches and lights and up-locks.

The corporal fitter has finished his checks. He grunts up from his perch behind the control column and tells me: 'She's all yours, sir. We had a bit of a mag drop on number three, earlier this afternoon; but we've cleared it. She's sweet as a bird, now.'

I sit in the left seat and begin my flight-deck ritual by adjusting the height for comfortable forward visibility. I take the handgrips of the control column and work the stick through full travels of simulated dive and climb. I twist the handwheel hard left and then hard right. Elevator and aileron controls are functional. I test the rudder pedals.

Roy Rheuben is in his navigation department in the nose section of the machine. Flight-Sergeant Rumming is examining the radar set and checking the workings of the wireless. His fellow tradesmen are variously ensuring that ammunition for the turret Brownings is in full supply and ready at hand, and that their intercom plugs are snugged home.

We test the communications system for clarity. All are united by voice.

I call to Ron Morse, in the engineer's cuddy behind me: 'Let's get the show moving. Turn on tanks one and three.'

'One and three on.'

I set the throttle of number one engine slightly open and the propeller control to increased revolutions. Carb-air intake is at cold. Radiator shutters are closed. The priming cock is turned on. I switch on the ignition and command Ron: 'Contact — port outer!'

Morse trips the switch of the starter magneto and presses the button of number one engine. By the light of the ground-crew torch we see the three-bladed propeller begin to turn, gathering revolutions. Then there is a flash of flame and a dragon-belch roar. And the engine has noisy life.

We move through the same steps until all the motors are running. There is now an exciting vibration running through Halifax B-Baker and it charges all of us with its electric energy.

While oil heats and begins to course through the engines' arteries, and as the pistons pulse at idling speed, I carry on with my observations. Checks, checks and checks! I look at temperatures and pressures and I lower and raise flaps until it is time to test the boost and magneto readings of each motor. I pull the stick hard back into my stomach and anchor the handwheel by clamping my left arm over it. I run up the port outer engine to fifteen hundred revolutions and check the magnetos. No fluctuation in the rev-readings. Good. And as the throttle is moved further forward I check the two-speed supercharger. Then I open up the engine, momentarily, to full take-off boost and revolutions. There is a savage tugging at the control column as the elevators are buffeted by angry, tormented air. And as I take off power to plus-nine boost I again check the magnetos.

Number three engine, the one that had shown a magneto drop earlier in the day, gets my careful attention. But it is fair enough, now. The mag-drop is less than one hundred revolutions on the gauge.

I wave away the wheel chocks. And when the flight sergeant below circles his torch and beckons me forward, I rumble the great machine on to the perimeter track and pick a cautious way along the rain-swept asphalt, following the blue pin-pricks of light that define a safe taxi-way.

We are at the end of the runway. I go through the painstaking procedures of final accounting. I signal the control tower, flashing the identity of our aircraft, seeking permission to scramble; and a flick of a switch in that department suddenly gives me an avenue of lights — my highway to the sky.

A bombing take-off is the most exciting part of flying. It is a manoeuvre to guide an aircraft, maximum-loaded with petrol and men and missiles, off a narrow strip of concrete or asphalt and safely wed the machine to the air. Often, as is the case tonight, the runway is icy and rain makes fanciful patterns on the windscreen. Always, it is accompanied by a full-powered bellow of engines. All the ingredients of drama are there — noise, tension and apprehension.

We career along between the row of lights. I have already checked the aircraft's predisposition to bear off to the left and the tail of the beast is up, so that I now have rudder control against the torque. Mark Twentyman, with his left hand following my right as I give steady, full travel to the throttles, has now taken care of the levers and has locked them with the damper in take-off setting. With his eyes on the gauges he chants his confidences in boost and engine-revolution output. I pull the Halifax off the runway at ninety-five knots and we climb away from Stornoway at 105 knots. All engines are rumbling sweetly. All little green-lit numerals and needles are dutifully aligned in their dials.

I motion my hand and tell my second-pilot: 'Undercart up!'

When the earth lies two or three hundred feet below us, I gradually take off the thirty-five degrees of flap I have used to give me added lift on take-off. We head along the course Roy Rheuben has given me for Cape Wrath, from which point we will steer eastward, through Pentland Firth and past Duncansby Head, towards Norway.

I say to Mark Twentyman: 'You can take her. I'm going for a look around.'

And my second-pilot edges himself behind the control column and assesses the readings of the instruments before him. There will not be a change of course for the next hour or more, so he engages 'George', our automatic pilot.

I make my way aft, checking with the boys at their respective posts. The radar scanner is completely functional. The wireless set is behaving itself. The turrets are swinging freely. And the Browning guns, having been tested by their operators, are firing without any stoppages. I move forward again and sit in the second-pilot's jump seat.

I stick my intercom plug into the socket and call to Rheuben, plotting away at his charts: 'Any problems?'

No. All is well in the navigation department.

From time to time the automatic pilot has to be checked against its few degrees of precession. Otherwise, it moves in its eerie way, the control column being eased forward or pulled back a trifling amount to counter climb or dive, the handwheel moving fractionally and continually to correct the ailerons. 'George', our invisible helmsman, is taking care of things with robot efficiency.

Twentyman and I sit and, sinfully, smoke our cigarettes.

We are nearing our ETA, our estimated time of arrival at Norway. I get back into my own seat and disengage the automatic pilot. We are now all acutely alert, and those of us on the flight deck or in the gun turrets peer into the blackness. We are at a height of one thousand feet and flying just below cloud. We have had intermittent rain ever since leaving Scotland. As is our custom, we have been flying without cabin lights, so that there will be no reflection on the windscreen to impair outside visibility.

Visibility for what? The night is as black as the grave. But any faint gleam of light. . .

Suddenly, wildly, I throw the aircraft on to its port wingtip; and there is, understandably, an immediate response from my travelling companions. 'What th' hell. . .?' Twentyman queries, his eyes wide and wild above his microphone mask.

'That orange light — dead ahead of us!' I gasp. 'Didn't you see it?'

Twentyman declared that he would be buggered if he did.

'As plain as I'm sitting here, it was. An orange light — moving in towards us. I was bloody sure we would collide.'

I call to the boys in the turrets: 'Any sign of a light out there at twelve o'clock — an orange light?'

No. The gunners have seen nothing. The dark heavens beyond and around us are untrammelled.

So I am dreaming? I am seeing one of the fabled, phantom lights that fly above the northern waters? Several of our squadron's pilots had reported sightings, adding their testimonies to the pile of claims from other units' airmen. Our assumptions were that the orange glows came from some type of electronic homing device fitted to German night-fighter aicraft. But the top brass of Coastal Command had continued to disclaim the existence of these lights. They were certainly not illuminations from enemy aircraft. In fact, the pundits stated, captured German aircrews had asked British intelligence what the strange orange lights had to do with our night-fighter tactics. A band of RAF intelligence officers from Coastal Command head-quarters came to our squadron and lectured us on the non-existence of this phenomenon. And the assembled aircrews drowned those declarations with cynical laughter.

We fly onwards. I have seen a ghost; and, since our aircraft's unprotected belly has not been raked by gunfire we are, presumably, safe so far from the Luftwaffe's night-fighters.

The enemy coast is not far distant. I engage the radio altimeter, setting the reading for two hundred feet and letting the aircraft descend on the amber light until the signal shows green. I now have a tolerance of ten feet either side of the two hundred feet height. If I let the aircraft sink lower than one hundred and ninety feet the signal will show a red warning glow. And lower than this lies eternity.

With my hands cautiously cosseting the control column we make our run for the shore. Rumming is on the radar set, reading the pattern of the land on the dial and telling of distance to gain. And on his warning I begin to climb. We get to one thousand feet and we are still in reasonably clear air. At two thousand feet we enter cloud and the magic of electric night puts on a pyrotechnic display for us. Our four propellers become circles of blue fire, rivalling in awesome beauty the most extravagant catherine wheels of our childhood fireworks festivals. Static electricity that we know as St. Elmo's fire is all around us, generated by the whirling blades of our airscrews and dancing between the muzzles of our Browning guns.

We are over our target area and we let down a hundred feet or more. Roy Rheuben lets go the first of our flares. We fly on until Wimpy Wellington in the rear turret calls that the chandeliers are ablaze; and we swing around to port and scan the fjord below us for signs of shipping. But in this waterway we have drawn a blank. The flares drift downwards, casting bright illumination over miles of wintery water and snow-cloaked hills, leaving ghostly trails of smoke until, one following the other, they die and the night is blacker than ever with their passing.

Not an angry shot has been fired at us.

'Next port of call,' I announce. And Roy Rheuben gives me directions.

We move southwards and follow the same procedure. But this time there is a hot reception awaiting us. Anti-aircraft fire is persistent but wide. We move around, hoping to see a target and praying escape from flak and night-fighters. But we see nothing and feel nothing, though we pry and peep into every corner of the flood-lit fjord. We continue our search in other areas.

Our supply of flares is exhausted. We return to the sea, which is our true element, and drop off height. Again, I rely on the advice of my radio altimeter and feel my way along the surface of the waves at two hundred feet. We may yet pick up an enemy ship travelling coastwise before our safety level of fuel is reached.

'Contact!' Lloyd Pollard, who is taking his trick on the radar scanner, has picked up something on the screen. 'Eight miles, dead ahead. A ship, medium size, by the looks of it!'

I have been flying a compass course of two hundred and sixty degrees. We are not very far from Alesund.

I check: 'It is not an island, is it?'

'No chance,' says Lloyd. 'It's long and sharp — just like a splinter of wood.' Then he calls to Rumming: 'Do you want to work it, Rum?'

The senior NCO and I both agree: 'No, you found him, so you take us on to him, Lloyd.'

Roy Rheuben is at his bombsight. And now begins a very close and meticulous liaison between him and Lloyd and me. The radar operator must guide us on to the target. The bomb aimer must, by stop-watch precision, know the distance run; and the pilot must be obedient, the faithful, non-swerving servant of his two team-mates.

It is time for me to climb to a safe bombing height. I power the Halifax to twelve hundred feet and begin our bombing run. We are very tense. I answer Rheuben's commands: 'Left-left. . . steady. . . r-i-g-h-t. . . steady, steady, keep her steady. . . s-t-e-a-d-y. . .' And then: '*Bombs gone!*'

There is a pregnant pause. And then, above the steady rumble of our Rolls-Royce engines comes a roll of explosions, and six yellow welts of light break the darkness below. The aircraft bucks and wallows in the blast as the bombs, with air-burst pistols, explode on the surface of the sea. We do not know if we have destroyed the target ship; that information will have to reach our intelligence officers later. But there is no point in lingering over the scene. A sinking ship would show on the radar screen just as would an undamaged vessel. So we cut and run towards home territory.

A Halifax of 502 Squadron on a night sortie at 200 feet.

Outside the vital danger area of Norwegian waters, I take the aircraft up to one thousand feet. I check our petrol supplies with Ron Morse and he tells me we are in good and fat shape. All four engines are running like silk and holding synchronization well. Even old 'George' does not seem inclined to precess so much. I sit back and relax.

Now is the time to eat our sandwich supper and drink our warm coffee. No baron's banquet ever tasted better — no wine, to celebrate a successful jousting, was more heady or vintage-blessed than the dark fluid in the vacuum flask.

I light a cigarette and watch 'George's' invisible hands commanding the control column. This wraith is truly an amazing fellow. The port wing dips; but, quick as a flash, the automatic pilot checks the erring aerofoil with uncanny logic. The nose of the Halifax drops in the turbulent air; and, again, there is an urgent correction-response made manifest by a backwards movement on the control column.

Carry on, you stout and noble flight companion!

We are winging homewards. It is another night, another sortie, almost behind us. Time slips blissfully in our wake and the beginnings of a new day grey the sky. Our landfall at Duncansby Head shows the land of Scotland a black silhouette against the lighter sea. On we fly to Cape Wrath; and down across North Minch we rumble to Tiumpan Head and the opening of Broad Bay. And we are over Stornoway in the early daylight.

We salute the control tower and receive permission to land. Our gear is down and Halifax B-Baker, seeking rest from our eleven-hour sortie, grumbles in over the dull harbour and the still-sleeping fisher folk. The wheels meet the runway surface and two puffs of blue-grey rubber smoke rise in the lazy air.

We run on until the brakes take control; then, with the two outer engines cut to facilitate taxying, we travel around the perimeter track to our dispersal point. We are ready for our debriefing session at operations room.

15
Return to Base

We were grieved to hear that Flight Lieutenant Taffy Evans had been killed at Aldergrove. He was the instructor of No 1674 Heavy Conversion Unit who had sent both Umpherson and myself off solo on our respective Halifax courses.

'He had just taken off with a trainee crew in one of the bloody old clapped-out Hallibags,' said our informant, a flying officer who had just arrived from Aldergrove, 'when he got a fire in his port-inner motor. It spread pretty quickly. The kite went in, in a mass of flames. It was a bloody awful sight. All in it were burned alive.'

We had heard the story so many times before that one would have thought we should be used to death. Well, perhaps we could get hardened somewhat to death when it was remote. But a fiery death. . . no, it was hard to take.

Not so long ago, for instance, a crew of Canadian lads had not returned from a Kattegat sortie. The fellow-countryman of some of the departed went through the dead men's gear, removing any evidence of clandestine sexual relationships (of which the grieving next-of-kin should never know), packing off to rightful claimants the personal belongings and displaying, for general consumption within the dormitory hut, the stockpiles of cigarettes, chocolate and soap cakes that the deceased had hoarded from their food parcels. We all helped ourselves, as the needs and the inclinations moved us, in a rather matter-of-fact manner. Death was a time for sharing. No man took his goodies with him to the grave. And the graves were, in this case, the remote deeps of a distant sea.

But Taffy Evans' passing hit us hard. Flames wreaked a terrible end, and it brought back memories of Howie Schraeder's pyre and Flight Sergeant Heyward's crash that exploded just two hundred metres from my tent at Burg el Arab. It reminded me too vividly, also, of Sergeant Vailland's blazing Maryland, and of other close shaves I had known in the Western Desert. In my mind's eye I could see Taffy, dazed and bruised, tearing at his safety straps and grappling frantically with the latch of the jammed escape hatch, fighting for his freedom beyond the buckled airframe and the fast-closing flames.

We continued to patrol the dark and misty air above the Scandinavian sea. Some aircraft returned with pepper-pot punctures ventilating their underbellies. Some came back unscathed. And some did not return. Our efforts were, in the main, successful. During November 1944 the squadron flew forty-four sorties and made nineteen attacks. The unit was doing a good job. Indeed, from the time and effort we put into our training, there was not much excuse for any shortcomings in our operational sorties.

Our crew was a close-knit band of brothers, a team of nine compatible fellows whose total efforts maintained our rating as an enthusiastic unit in the squadron. There was no hint of discord. Twentyman had long resigned himself to his stint as second-joe; and I suspect he was even developing a sneaking regard for the once despised Halifax.

Additional to our training stooges over the waters of the North Minch, a bombing school had been set up at Leuchars, close by St. Andrews in Fifeshire, Scotland. And we were sent there, crew by crew on roster, to become skilled in the latest techniques of missile-dropping.

It was while we were there that I experienced my one difficult experience in getting a Halifax back to earth without bending anything. We were on a night practice-bombing exercise, flying reliable old HR815 U-Uncle one bleak December night. Take-off had been achieved satisfactorily from an icy runway and we covered the target area, run by run, and dropped our sticks of eleven-and-a-half pounders in fast-closing weather. As we completed the programme and stood towards base, we were slightly apprehensive of the snow that was falling fast and of the wind that we knew, from our observations over the bombing range, was strengthening and blowing from a different quarter.

We came up on the airfield and called for permission to land. The control tower gave us our barometric pressure and the runway we were to use. The WAAF girl, with well-rounded vowels, warned us of snow and ice and told us of a strong cross-wind. Oh, happy night!

The flarepath came alight and I made an exploratory run up and over the runway at a thousand feet to align my gyro-compass and assess drift. Twentyman and I peered through the swirling snowstorm. We made our ninety-degree turn across wind and pressed onwards for a minute or so before coming on to the down-wind heading of one hundred and eighty degrees on the gyro. I dropped the undercart and a few degrees of flap. But when we looked to port to find some trace of the airfield, we saw only blackness. The storm had blotted out everything that could have been a marker for us.

We turned towards the down-wind end of the runway, dropping height to seven hundred feet and giving the Halifax full flaps. And when I thought it was time to turn, I banked to port for the final run in. But there was no sign of the flarepath. Twentyman and I shot swift glances at each other before our eyes dropped instinctively to the altimeter. I let the machine slide lower and I squinted out of the darkened cockpit into the blizzard.

Then Mark Twentyman called: 'There, there!' And as he spoke I, too, saw the threshold of the dim avenue of lights four hundred feet below us — but bearing about about thirty degrees to our left. We were getting a lot of starboard drift. I gave U-Uncle the gun, took up the undercarriage and left about thirty-five degrees of flap hanging down so that we could grope around slowly in precautionary flight. I lined up on the fast disappearing runway lights and made another attempt to bring a landing-circuit to a happy conclusion.

The cross-wind was strong and it came from a quarter that was somewhere between the directions of the Leuchars runways. Whichever landing strip had been selected by Flying Control, it would still be quite a few degrees away from the eye of the strong wind.

I had to make another attempt at trying to line up my Halifax on the flarepath before I finally managed to battle through the snowstorm and set the wheels down safely on the runway. The Flying Control WAAF in the tower called: 'U-Uncle, you are clear to taxi to dispersal. Follow the van. There is a strong wind from 0-four-0. Be careful of snow. There is ice on the runway. Over!'

My dear girl, now that we are down, we don't care if all the earth and hell itself freezes over.

The Airfield Control van bustled up to us with a waving of torches. It U-turned in front of us and showed its big illuminated 'Follow Me' sign — an invitation I accepted most gladly. I cut my outboard engines and motored U-Uncle on the two inboards for ease of manoeuvrability, throttling and braking our way to the aeroplane's dispersal point. The gale slammed against the aircraft's twin rudders and those big wind surfaces kicked against me in protest, making my feet strain on the pedals.

It was while we were at Leuchars that I had a recurrence of the violent stomach pains that had, from time to time, plagued me since the attacks first began in the Western Desert. My weight, hardly superfluous since my illness while at Malta, had begun to fall away again. So I was dispatched to Gleneagles, the internationally famous Perthshire hotel, which had been taken over as a military hospital. I swallowed bowls of barium meal and was X-ray photographed in various poses. I was required to gulp down a rubber tube through which samples of my stomach juices were drawn for analysis. I remained at Gleneagles for about two weeks while doctors observed my gut's antics. And the prescribed cure to alleviate my discomfort was hydrochloric acid, diluted with water and sipped daily.

Time and the tide of war moved on. In March 1945 Dorothy had an official message from London advising her that her name was on the list for early embarkation for New Zealand. So I made an application through my commanding officer for my repatriation, so that I could either travel with her or at least be in New Zealand to greet her on her arrival. I had been away from my country for about four years. Wing Commander H H C Holderness, who had assumed command of 502 Squadron in November 1944, was most co-operative and gave his official approval.

My crew and I flew one or two sorties while I awaited the decisions of the RAF and the RNZAF authorities. Out of the blackness that so often veiled the Kattegat we could see, on a clear night, the bright lights of Göteborg in Sweden and, southwards, the glow that came from Copenhagen. Mark Twentyman and I vowed that we would never attempt to nurse a battered aircraft back the long and storm-wracked miles to Britain while there was a chance of setting the machine down in neutral Sweden or Denmark.

For my old Halifax crew mates there was to be fulfilment of that vow. Not long after I had got my repatriation clearance from the squadron and the RAF, they were flying with their new skipper, Flying Officer Peter Davenport, on a Kattegat sortie when their aircraft developed a fault.

A recent letter from my ex-navigator Roy Rheuben in Reno, USA, explains the circumstances and the subsequent adventures that befell the nine lads in strange territory. Roy's words are quoted:

'The patrol took place just after VE Day. I understand that all German U-boats had been ordered to surface and then proceed to certain designated ports. Our patrol that day, over the North Sea, Skagerrak and Kattegat, was primarily a surveillance flight to chart any U-boat we spotted and to ensure it was on its correct heading. It was whilst we were in the Kattegat area that we developed a main hydraulic fracture. And after communicating this matter to base, we were ordered to land at the nearest airfield — which happened to be Copenhagen — and await the arrival of another RAF aircraft which would bring us mechanics and the necessary spare parts.

'I recall that the hydraulic fracture was such that the undercarriage could not be lowered in the conventional manner but had to be wound down by hand. We were to be in Copenhagen three days before the repair crew could render the Halifax airworthy again.

'At the Copenhagen airfield we found that a courier RAF aircraft had already preceded us with the necessary personnel to take over duties in the control tower. They, poor souls, were of course confined to duty at the airfield while we had no tasks but to await the completion of repairs to our aircraft. So we eagerly accepted their arrangements of transport to, and accommodation in, one of the major hotels in downtown Copenhagen. This being just two days after the VE Day formalities, Allied troops had not yet been dispatched this far north to take over from the occupying German troops. So I must say it was somewhat disconcerting, if not unnerving, to encounter on the streets so many German soldiers who still carried rifles over their shoulders while I was armed with nothing more potent than my navigation pencil.

'Nor were my feelings groundless, as we were to discover the next day when we returned to the airfield. About four of us spotted some German Me-109f fighter planes parked at a distance corner of the field and curiosity prompted us to walk over and climb up to peer into the cockpits. After a few minutes we had started to walk back towards the control tower when there was the sudden report of a rifle shot and the sound of a bullet ricochet much too close for comfort. Needless to say, we hit the dirt immediately and stayed down for a minute or two before hastening over to the control tower.

'I can see where, had the shoe been on the other foot, many of us would have been tempted to get in just one more shot at the enemy before having to surrender our weapons.

'On the first evening at the hotel, whilst partaking of a glass or three of schnapps in the lobby, we were taken in tow by several members of the Royal Danish Opera Company who guided us on a tour of the city, winding up at the Royal Opera House (no performance that particular night) where we were treated to a ride up in the plush royal elevator leading to the even more plush royal box. We had a great evening with that most friendly group and, after a few more glasses of schnapps, we had no difficulty in persuading them to give forth with their operatic endeavours.

'On one of our afternoons in Copenhagen we were introduced to several members of the Danish Underground, who took us on a tour around the outskirts of the city and showed us a house which had been the hub of their meetings and the location of their arms during the German occupation. There was nothing unusual about the appearance of the place, but it seemed to be just a little too close to a nearby German barracks for comfort. But perhaps it was that cocky proximity which enabled it to remain undetected by the Germans.

'Even if so many Danes seemed intent on giving us the red carpet treatment, I never thought I would see the day when I would be besieged by people asking for my autograph. This occurred to two or three of us one day when we went into one of the larger stores hoping to buy a souvenir or two to take home. After signing my name quite a number of times, I began to wonder if there was a shorter name I could scribble. So, to this day, there may exist in Copenhagen several autographs of a certain Flying Officer Tom Mix.

'Our final night (or early morning) was marred by the sounding of a fire alarm which awakened us and sent us hurrying to the downstairs lobby. After about half-an-hour the firemen announced that those whose rooms were not on the same level as the fire's outbreak could safely return to slumber. The seat of the blaze was in a room on the fifth floor. We were sleeping immediately below.

'Later, after a hurried breakfast, we had to leave for the airfield, as we had been told that our aircraft was ready for flight. We were somewhat disappointed that our hasty departure precluded the opportunity to get the full story on the hotel fire. So we will never know whether the blaze was accidental, or the deliberate act of some disgruntled German who perhaps had an overly warm reception in mind for the hotel's Allied guests.'

★ ★ ★

I left Stornoway as one of fifteen passengers in Halifax E-Easy in transit to Doncaster. Flight Lieutenant Townshend was the pilot — my last link, that day, with 502 Squadron. Soon after that, on 25 May 1945 to be precise, the unit was deactivated at Stornoway, its wartime duties well performed.

I was sent to Brighton and into the care of No 12 (RNZAF) PDRC. Soon I was aboard the troopship *Empress of Scotland*, bound for New Zealand by way of Sydney. For me the war was over. I had survived the hazards of the air over various seas and landscapes, and had walked away from five serious prangs. With nothing in my pockets, I had, with sublime confidence in my abilities, persuaded an English girl to marry me and follow me into an unknown future. Neither of us had any doubts about our tomorrows. I was reasonably healthy and, albeit a bit battered, mobile enough for the peacetime jungle. Life, I decided, had been exceeding kind to me, and luck had favoured me passing fair.

My crews? A pilot who had dependents aboard his aircraft lives with a great responsibility. Thank God, I have never crashed a man to his death, nor yet have I injured any of my flying companions, save bruising a dignity or two. Dutton and Norman had sweated out their apprehensions on several occasions, but managed to emerge safely from the predicaments they shared with me.

Les Norman, my first navigator — look down from your Valhalla and tell me what life could have given you, had you survived that ditching off the island of Gavdhos. Today, you would have been a man in his sixties. Married, undoubtedly, because you were a handsome lad with an eye for a fetching figure and a fair face. And your children would be married, no doubt, and in their turn giving to the world their seed.

Les, I wish you had not flown with another crew on that dark day in 1942.

And did you get home from Malta unharmed, Ces Dutton? The years have gone and time has closed over us.

Sonny Cliffe and Andy Covich were fit and well when they returned to New Zealand. We sat and yarned of old times when we were reunited in Auckland years ago. But Time the Reaper came along and first Sonny and then Andy went. Thorpe, our Australian fourth member of the Baltimore crew, was killed somewhere along the way of war, after he had served his stint on Malta.

All of my Halifax crew survived the war. But well over forty years since we last flew together, only three of us are still corresponding. Roy Rheuben is a doctor of dentistry with his own practice in Reno, Nevada. We last saw him in late 1970 when Dorothy, our son Mike and I were guests of Roy and Ellen Rheuben when we travelled through the United States.

Tom (Wimpy) Wellington, one of our Australian WOP-AGs, returned to his home in Ayr, Northern Queensland, after the war and spent the rest of his working life with the Queensland Post Office Service. He is now retired and lives at Surfers Paradise, Queensland.

Lloyd Pollard died in New South Wales in the late 1970s. We continue to correspond with his widow Norma who, like Dorothy, is English. And Ron Morse, our flight engineer, became a civil engineer and had his home at Walton-on-Thames. He died in the early 1980s and we continue to exchange letters and cards with his widow Grace.

And the others — Mark Twentyman, Blackie Sharp, Rum Rumming and Safe Keeping? Alas, with the passing of the years they have disappeared without trace.

16

Dispersal Point

I had been settled in civilian life for about two years when I was attracted by a newspaper advertisement that invited applications for volunteer weekend service in the RNZAF Territorial Squadrons which were being reorganised.

Although I thought I was probably a bit too old to be considered, I wrote away for an entry form, gave the necessary particulars of my service history, and forgot about the affair. But before long I was called before a selection board, and I was also required to undergo a standard pilot medical check. Again I let the matter slide out of mind, reckoning that keen young ex-pilots would be thick on the ground and that my chances of selection would be slight. Already, I was two years over the required age limit.

But one night just before the new year of 1949 was born, there came a heavy rapping on my front door. The time must have been close to midnight, and the sight of a policeman with a torch in one hand and a document in the other was disturbing.

He checked if he had the right household; and then he handed me an OHMS telegram and asked me to sign receipt of it. I found I had been selected Flight Commander of Bomber Flight, 1 (Auckland) Territorial Squadron, RNZAF.

It is, of course, academic that 1 Squadron never came anywhere near having a Bomber Flight, in spite of the loftiest official intentions when the Air Force Territorial Scheme was resurrected in late 1948. The penurious state of the Government's defence budget was to become manifest — or as manifest as the great public can ever know —

as time progressed. But we reported, bird-bright and chock-full of enthusiasm, at Whenuapai and met our fellow fortunates. We were issued with our khaki drill and our battle-dress uniforms and saw, too, the nucleus of our squadron's fleet of aircraft — two little DH-82 Tiger Moths.

The late Keith Paterson, with the rank of squadron leader, was our commanding officer. My fellow flight commanders were Don Clow, who was to lead Fighter Flight, and Jack Elmsley, who was to be responsible for the workings of Training Flight. Flight Lieutenant Jack Fox was to be our navigation leader and Flight Lieutenant Bill Tremayne had been selected as engineer officer.

Flight Lieutenant Bill Ziesler of the regular Air Force was our squadron adjutant, flying instructor, guide and mentor. Bill was later killed in an air accident in the South Island.

After landing the Halifax machines from my cockpit perch about twenty-five feet above the runway, I found the little Tiger Moths ridiculously sensitive on the controls and disconcertingly low to the ground. On the first dual landing I found myself levelling for touch-down about a dozen feet too high. And after some familiarization turns, stalls, spins and circuits and bumps, I was sent off solo and urged the gentle aircraft into steep turns, side-slips and forced landings.

It was a matter of history repeating itself. It was from that same airfield, eight years earlier, that I had, unassisted, climbed a Tiger Moth off the grass sward and so opened the first chapter of my saga of flight.

It was not long before the squadron took delivery of two more Tiger Moths, and we were able to extend our repertoire of aerial tricks to include pilot-navigation exercises, in which the hard-working driver did sums with feverish concentration and committed his calculations to a flight-log pad strapped to his thigh. The rain beat into the open cockpit and the slipstream tore at the sheets of the flight-log. And the little aeroplanes of canvas, wood and wire bucked and wallowed, just as the magnificent flying machine built by Wilbur and Orville Wright must have battled with the turbulences of the new element upon which man had intruded.

As good and reliable as we voted Mr de Havilland's little gem, it was not long before we inherited our first Harvard trainer, and were rejoicing in our aerial progress. Whereas the other pilots of our squadron had had earlier training in those aircraft, I had graduated from Tiger Moths on to Airspeed Oxford two-engined machines and had continued my flying in multi-engined aircraft. So I found myself involved in all the fighter pilot's tactics in miniature. Loops, spins, peel-offs, rolls, climbing turns and curves of pursuit made up the normal weekend flying programme. And there was a bit of low flying injected into the syllabus by most of us. It was strictly illegal, except when practised over defined, non-populated areas. But I did, on more than one occasion when I had omitted to wear my wrist watch, fly down over Auckland City low enough for me to see the time on the Town Hall clock.

The late Tommy Beech, then one of our non-commissioned pilots, created a bit of a furore when he flew low into some electric-power lines and so cut off fuel and light from the Kumeu district for a few hours. Happily, Tommy was quite uninjured and his machine was but slightly bent.

If we were providing the nucleus of an auxiliary force of volunteer airmen ready to defend the realm, the citizens of Auckland, as a whole, seemed to take a decidedly dim view of our weekend activities.

A Harvard of 1 Squadron, RNZAF.

There were complaints in plenty when I flew a Harvard around the gun emplacements on North Head one Sunday morning during an Army co-operation exercise. The Harvard, in all fairness to the citizens of Devonport, emitted a particularly abrasive din when under a power load. It was suggestive of a circular saw cutting through a sheet of roofing iron. So, not surprisingly, the several letters to the editors of Auckland's newspapers were unanimous in discouraging the squadron from further manoeuvres of that nature.

We had our annual camps at Ohakea, and I was able to spread my hitherto folded Bomber Flight wings and become reacquainted with the two-engined Oxfords again, luring our navigators into the air, and leaning on their dead-reckoning findings while the fighter boys played with their curves of pursuit and their aerial gunnery exercises.

We pottered around the skyways of greater Auckland for about three years, devoting most of our weekends to parades at Whenuapai. Fighter Flight was fortunate in gaining the use of several Mustang fighters that had been stored at Ardmore airfield. But the bombers that had been planned for 1 Squadron never materialized. The unit, in fact, did not progress beyond the Mustang stage, although the pilots in the latter months of the squadron's existence as a Territorial body did receive training on Vampire jet fighters.

Squadron Leaders Ralph Court and Skip Watson were, successively, commanding officers of the enthusiastic little 1 (Auckland) Territorial Squadron after Keith Paterson's reign ended, Keith and his flight commanders stepping down after our three-year term ended in December 1951.

The life of the re-born Territorial Air Force as a whole was short. With the war won a few years earlier, and with a new Government in office since the resurrection of the Territorial scheme, the four squadrons based respectively in Auckland, Wellington, Christchurch and Dunedin, were disbanded in 1957.

So this, pressed into the compass of less than a dozen years, has been an important part of my life. If I hold the door open for the memories that have warmed me through some of the colder, more uncharitable days, I beckon around me the moments of companionship and endeavour that have truly counted. And I am rich.

Those fragments of time have been earned in cockpits redolent of the sweat of tension, of oil and high-octane petrol. Or I have won them in the safe harbours of crew rooms and desert tents and Nissen huts. They have been earned — because one cannot buy the friendships of Webster and Papps and Keys. The loyalty of Cliffe and Covich, of Rheuben and Wellington, Pollard and Morse is not measured in money. And there is no buying the power and the glory of flight beneath a star-scattered sky, or the sovereignty of a small doman held poised 'twixt wind and water.

Wind and water. The yang and the yin of my Air Force life!

Within the short passage of time between 1940 and 1952 I grew wings and flew far. I knew real fear — too many times — and I found firm friends. And, alas, I saw many of them die. I met a dear woman and we married and brought new and precious life into this world.

So life goes on. Brave trees fall to the storms, seeds are sown and young saplings grow to take their places. But, time upon time we realize that we shall never again hear the voice of a friend as, one by one, our companions drift away.

'The war took a lot out of your life,' some well-meaning people used to say to me, years ago, when I was sorting myself out in post-war civilian life. 'You missed out on some good opportunities in the business world.'

Did I? It is all a matter of swings and roundabouts, I believe. There were gains and losses — and some of those gains I would not trade for the wealth of some of the richest stay-at-home barons. My wife would ascribe events as Fate. I have wanted many things in life, and I believe I have fulfilled more of my desires than I have missed, because there is a strange but undeniable law of life that moves us inexorably towards that which our hearts truly desire.

I wanted to fly. I was drawn to it as, compulsively, our godwits must wing their ways to Siberia without knowing the why and the wherefore. I had no lust to kill; nor did I march forward chanting anthems and waving a flag high. I was patriotic, but not a fanatic. A glove of challenge was thrown down. It might have been an academic degree to be gained or an athletic trophy to be won. Or it might have been the same tugging force that drew Hillary to Everest or Scott to the South Pole.

Along with all the professors, the athletes and the explorers, along with the thousands of my contemporaries, I followed a gleam and I climbed towards the stars.

Index